THE LUCCHESE
MAFIA CRIME FAMILY

The Complete History of a New York Criminal Organization (Five Families)

MAFIA LIBRARY

© **Copyright 2023 - All rights reserved.**

The content contained within this book may not be reproduced, duplicated or transmitted without direct written permission from the author or the publisher.

Under no circumstances will any blame or legal responsibility be held against the publisher, or author, for any damages, reparation, or monetary loss due to the information contained within this book, either directly or indirectly.

Legal Notice:

This book is copyright protected. It is only for personal use. You cannot amend, distribute, sell, use, quote or paraphrase any part, or the content within this book, without the consent of the author or publisher.

Disclaimer Notice:

Please note the information contained within this document is for educational and entertainment purposes only. All effort has been executed to present accurate, up to date, reliable, complete information. No warranties of any kind are declared or implied. Readers acknowledge that the author is not engaged in the rendering of legal, financial, medical or professional advice. The content within this book has been derived from various sources. Please consult a licensed professional before attempting any techniques outlined in this book.

By reading this document, the reader agrees that under no circumstances is the author responsible for any losses, direct or indirect, that are incurred as a result of the use of the information contained within this document, including, but not limited to, errors, omissions, or inaccuracies.

TABLE OF CONTENTS

Introduction 1

Chapter 1 : Forging A Crime Family: Beginnings 5
    Origins Of The American Mafia 5
    The Morello Gang And Gaetano Reina 9
    The Castellammarese War 14
    A Switch Of Allegiance 15

Chapter 2 : Trouble Doubled: The Two Tommies 19
    Formation Of The Five Families 19
    Unseating The Capo Di Tutti Capi 22
    Tommy Gagliano 25

Chapter 3 : Power And Profit: The Lucchese Era 29
    The Lucchese Namesake 29
    Political Maneuvers 32
    The Lucchese-Gambino Alliance 36

Chapter 4 : International Smuggling: Carmine "Mr. Gribbs" Tramunti And The French Connection 41
    Carmine Tramunti 42
    The French Connection 44
    Trading Places 47

Chapter 5 : "Tony Ducks": The Reign Of Anthony Corallo 51
Anthony Corallo 51
The Family Under Corallo 55
Bugging The Jaguar 57
The Mafia Commission Trial 59

Chapter 6 : A Ruthless Stranglehold: Vittorio Amuso And Anthony Casso 65
Amuso And Casso 66
The Duo With Iron Fists 69
The Mafia Cops 74
A Boss And Underboss Captured 76

Chapter 7 : The Boss Of Snitches: Alphonse "Little Al" D'arco 79
Alphonse "Little Al" D'arco 80
Installment As Acting Boss 83
Facilitating Murder 85
Boss-Turned-Informant 87

Chapter 8 : Shifting Leadership: The Era Of Acting Bosses 93
Joseph "Little Joe" Defede 94
Steven Crea 96
Louis "Louie Bagels" Daidone 100
A Change In Tactic 102

Chapter 9 : Taking Back Power: The Ruling Panel And Matthew Madonna 103
A Panel Of Three 104
Madonna Takes Over 106

 Bombarded With Charges 108

 The Leadership Topples 111

Chapter 10 : Ran From Behind Bars: The "Modern" Lucchese Crime Family 113

 The New Hierarchy 114

 Continuing Criminal Investigations 117

 The Lucchese Crime Family Today 120

Conclusion 123

References 127

INTRODUCTION

Since the creation of the five families, the Lucchese borgata had proved to be the most stable and least divisive of the New York families.

–**Selwyn Raab**

The ideas of organized crime and the Mafia are some that many in our society would claim to be well versed in. Considering the rise and continued popularity of organized crime in media (*Goodfellas* and *The Departed* from director Martin Scorsese and HBO's television show *The Sopranos,* to name but a few), it is understandable that one who consumes this content would believe that they were knowledgeable in the intricacies of organized crime and the self-made gangsters that lead these groups. In this media, underdog protagonists create or join crime groups to rise up in society, benefiting from the power and wealth that this affords them and finding themselves in often violent scuffles to remain on top. These protagonists are usually framed as flawed but honorable, headstrong but well-mannered, and arguably garner a great deal of sympathy from the audience.

However, while there is absolutely no suggestion being made here that these fictional accounts of organized crime shown on film and television do not draw from real events, organizations, and individuals in their content, their often romanticized nature can overshadow the very real organizations that inspired them. The true nature of organized crime is wholly complex and very often brutal. While no ire should be aimed at fictionalized stories shown in media, which are expected to expand kernels of truth with creative license to create an engaging story, it is important to remind oneself that these stories are based on very real crime organizations that have had and continue to have a stranglehold on society through violence, coercion, and expansive criminal enterprises.

Throughout the 20th century, numerous mafia organizations rose to power, carving out spheres of control, influence, and power all over the United States. From the cacophony of emerging criminal enterprise came one organization, however, that stands out from the rest: the Lucchese crime family. Indeed, from the above quote by American journalist Selwyn Raab (considered an expert on the subject of the American Mafia), we can catch a glimpse of the respect and infamy garnered by the Lucchese crime family. There are many aspects that separate the Lucchese crime family from its contemporaries. Firstly, its diametric personality as both a relatively peaceful organization but also one that instituted one of the most violent reigns in American Mafia history. Secondly, its varied cast of Bosses and other individuals who ranged from an acting Boss that made the ultimate betrayal to a powerful duo who murdered nearly everyone who dared to cross them. Finally, its position as a respected member of the infamous Five Families who organized, controlled, and oversaw the majority of criminal enterprise in the United States. In this book, these aspects of the Lucchese crime family will be explored, amongst others, showcasing the impact and influence of the organization on both the burgeoning criminal enterprises of the early 20th century United States as well as in the modern day.

Before this exploration begins, it seems rather fitting to segue into the main body of it with a quote from Charles "Lucky" Luciano, considered to be instrumental in the rise of organized crime in the United States, to show the prevailing philosophy of those engaged in organized mafia crime: "There's no such thing as good money or bad money. There's just money" ("Lucky Luciano," n.d.).

CHAPTER 1
FORGING A CRIME FAMILY: BEGINNINGS

Of course, just like the large majority of the other criminal organizations that found their beginnings in the boiling pot of New York City in the early 20th century, the Lucchese crime family did not manifest into being a fully-fledged criminal organization with extensive spheres of influence. Instead, there were many aspects, both social and political, that served as catalysts for the organization's eventual rise to power. In this chapter, we will explore the aspects that led to the formation of what would later become the Lucchese crime family, from the origins of the organized mafia in the United States to the small criminal gang that nurtured individuals that would go on to create the most infamous of Mafia families, including the man who would come to be known as the first Boss of the Lucchese crime family.

Origins of the American Mafia

Pinpointing the exact origin of the American Mafia is, at the very best, extremely difficult. At worst, the task is nigh impossible, mainly due to the essence of organized crime in general. Indeed, by its very nature, organized crime propagates most effectively when operating in the shadows of society. Despite the examples of various mafia bosses acting to the contrary (that is doing very little to hide their criminal and often violent activities and, in the most extreme cases, flaunting them for the world to see), these examples are contextual to their time. They occured much later when the American Mafia had successfully cemented their power and influence, therefore making it much harder for law enforcement agencies to access and imprison.

In the early 20th century, however, the pockets of organized crime gangs spread across the United States did not have the luxury of putting themselves in the firing line of law enforcement. Instead, they operated in the undercurrent of society in order to grow and consolidate their influence. Hence, the early history of organized crime within the United States remains frustratingly cryptic. In his book *American Mafia: A History of its Rise to Power*, Thomas Reppetto (2009) paints an accurate overview of the inception of the Mafia in the United States: "An account of the rise of the American Mafia is more than just a crime story. It is a window into American society illustrating the workings of political, governmental, bureaucratic, and economic forces" (p. 6).

With this in mind, one may reasonably be pondering on who made up these early criminal gangs that would later coalesce and transform into the complex mafia organizations we see operating from the mid-20th century through to the present day. A prevailing and widely accepted opinion of the make-up of these early criminal gangs were solely of Italian (or, more specifically, Sicilian) descent. Indeed, a newspaper article from *The New Orleans Times* in 1869 pervaded this opinion when it stated that a district of the city had "been infested by well-known and notorious Sicilian murderers, counterfeiters, and burglars that [have] formed a sort of general co-partnership or stock company for the plunder and disturbance of the city" (Tosches, 2013). The bias shown in this article was adopted by the American public, who began "[using] the word *Mafia* as shorthand for the Italian-dominated organized crime groups" (Reppetto, 2009, p.2). Reppetto (2009) suggests that this opinion, however, "is misleading," as it "places too much emphasis on foreign organizations and alien conspiracies," feeding into the historical "anti-immigrant sentiment" that permeated American society at this time (pp. 2–3).

In some senses, Reppetto's suggestion is accurate. Many criminal gangs operating at the turn of the 20th century in the United States were steeped in the heritage of various ethnic backgrounds. New York City (widely thought to be the center point in the rise of the American Mafia) was a city "where nearly three-quarters of the inhabitants were either immigrants or children of immigrants" (Reppetto, 2009, p.27). Those of Italian heritage were most definitely a large percentage of the population, with the number of Italians in the city "leaping from 20,000 to 250,000" from 1880 to 1900, but they still remained only "the fourth-largest immigrant group" behind the Irish, German, and Jewish populations (Reppetto, 2009, p.27). Due to the poor socioeconomic standing of immigrants at this time, many individuals formed small organizations in order to change their fortunes and, consequently, find a much more lucrative enterprise than anything the United States government could offer them. These organizations comprised many ethnic heritages and were not solely those of Italian descent. This is why Reppetto (2009) prefers the use of the term "American Mafia," as it "conveys the reality that Italian-dominated gangs arose primarily out of socioeconomic conditions in this country [the United States] and often worked in partnership with mobsters from other ethnic backgrounds" (p. 3).

While it is abundantly clear that the stereotype that those of Italian descent are somehow predisposed to violent and criminal behaviors was fuelled by the racist and xenophobic attitudes that permeated the United States at this time, there is still a strong link between the criminal gangs that would eventually amalgamate into the infamous Mafia crime families and Italian heritage.

One reason for this link may be born from the aforementioned socioeconomic plight of the lower classes in the United States. The ethnic classes of the late 19th and early 20th centuries of the United States occupied the lowest rungs of social class. The "ethnic succession" argument posits that "as the Irish and other groups moved into the middle classes, they were less likely to be represented in criminal activity," hence the later arrival of Italian immigrants "filled the void" (Reppetto, 2009, pp. 3–4). In other words, the Irish, German, and Jewish immigrants, who populated New York City long before the Italians arrived, managed to ascend the social ladder, leaving a space in the lower classes that the newly arriving Italian immigrants had to fill. This "natural succession" was further exacerbated by the attitudes of New York City law enforcement who, instead of creating actionable plans to combat the crime-riddled lower-class areas of the city, were content with all but ignoring the problem, choosing instead to funnel the arriving Italian immigrants into poor areas, effectively ghettoizing them (Reppetto, 2009, p. 3).

Another reason focuses on the very culture of southern Italian criminals', who had a very "business-like approach" to criminal activity (Reppetto, 2009, p. 30). Where the non-Italian criminal gangs, who were "largely just extensions of street gangs," operated in a chaotic, unruly, and violent manner, the Italian criminal leaders "eschewed senseless mayhem in favor of more rational methods" (Reppetto, 2009, p. 30). When the leaders of the non-Italian gangs were imprisoned or killed, "their organizations usually collapsed," while when the Italian leaders "passed from the scene, their organizations remained, lasting to the present" (Reppetto, 2009, p. 31).

Despite this look at the origins of organized crime in the United States being somewhat of a whistlestop tour on the subject, one now has a foundation of knowledge on the landscape in which the criminal gangs operated and grew from. One of these gangs would be essential in the nurturing of many important individuals who would go on to lead the most powerful of the Mafia crime families in the United States, including the Lucchese crime family: the Morello gang.

The Morello Gang and Gaetano Reina

Around 1892, a young Sicilian named Giuseppe Morello arrived in the United States. Hailing from a family of mobsters, Morello was all too familiar with criminal enterprise before arriving in New York City, traveling there to escape Sicilian law enforcement. Morello had been suspected of the murder of Giovanni Vella, "the head of a quasi-police force called the *Guardie Campestri*" (Bruno, 2022). Additionally, Morello's counterfeiting ring had recently been uncovered, with Morello himself being caught and arrested with "a fistful of phony cash" prior to his escape to the United States (Bruno, 2022).

One physical characteristic served his criminal undertakings well, as Morello was "born with a severely deformed right hand with only an elongated pinkie finger bent grotesquely downwards" (Bruno, 2022). Due to this deformity, Morello came to be known by many names, including "The Clutch Hand" and "Little Finger," adding to his imposing and often brutal nature within the criminal underworld. Soon after his arrival to the United States, his family joined him: Bernardo Terranova (notorious Sicilian gangster and Morello's stepfather), his mother Angelina, his sister Maria, four of his step-siblings (three half-brothers and one half-sister), as well as his wife and infant son. For a time, Morello and his family "tried their best to fly under the radar of American law enforcement," moving from New York City to Louisiana, then to Texas, and finally back to New York City in 1897 (Bruno, 2022).

Around the time of Morello's resettlement in New York City, another young Sicilian with a talent for criminal activity arrived stateside. His name was Ignazio Lupo, and he was on the run from Sicilian law enforcement after fatally shooting business rival Salvatore Morello (no relation to Giuseppe Morello). Settling in New York City at the turn of the 20th century, Lupo went into business running numerous shopfronts, one of which was a saloon at 8 Prince Street in Lower Manhattan. The two Sicilian outlaws would inevitably meet when, in 1902, Morello acquired a separate saloon that operated out of the rear of 8 Prince Street. With this, the beginning of the Morello gang was put in position as Morello and

Lupo began "a series of illegal endeavors, most of which terrorized the Italian immigrants of New York City" (Bruno, 2022).

Lupo did not hesitate to align himself closely with Morello and his family. In 1903, Lupo married Morello's half-sister Salvatrice Terranova, solidifying his link to Morello. Although their partnership operated various criminal enterprises, two in particular proved rather profitable for the pair: Black Hand extortion and counterfeiting. Morello and Lupo would send extortion letters to local businessmen, threatening them with the "bombing of their businesses or even death if the businessman did not immediately cough up some very substantial cash" (Bruno, 2022). These letters were not empty threats, with one local butcher who refused to pay the $1,000 extortion price being murdered in cold blood when "two men marched into his butcher shop and shot [him] dead" (Bruno, 2022). The pair also ran a large counterfeiting operation "originating in the sleepy upstate town of Highland, New York, 50 miles from New York City" (Bruno, 2022). Both the extortion and counterfeiting schemes were aided by Lupo's "wholesale network of grocery stores," which acted as fronts for the duo's illicit enterprises. The success of Morello and Lupo's criminal activities came grinding to a halt, however, when, in 1910, they were arrested on counterfeiting charges and sentenced to 25 years and 30 years in prison.

With its two helmsmen behind bars, the Morello gang fell into disarray. All three of Morello's step-brothers (Nicholas, Vincenzo, and Ciro) took leadership of the gang at various times through conflicts such as the two-year Mafia-Camorra War from 1915–1917 and, in 1920, both Morello and Lupo were released from prison and rejoined the leadership of the gang. However, Salvatore D'Aquila, a former captain of the Morello gang, had branched out during the organization's destabilized period and was considered Manhattan's Mafia Boss. Realizing that his position of power could now be challenged, D'Aquila engaged the Morello gang in a brutal turf war that did not end until many lives had been snuffed out. As the dust of this conflict began to clear, the Morello gang's transition into what would later be known as the Genovese crime family whirred into motion. As interesting as this period in the American Mafia's history is, one may be wondering as to its relevance to the main focus of this exploration: the Lucchese crime family. As the Morello gang expanded its influence and power across New York City and the surrounding areas, a mobster by the name of Gaetano Reina was rising along with the organization.

Born in 1889, Reina grew up in Corleone, Sicily, with his father Giacomo, mother Carmela, and brother Antonio. Immigrating to the United States in the early 1900s, Reina and his family settled in the East Harlem neighborhood of New York City. Not long after their arrival, Reina and his brother fell into working with members of the Morello crime family. Despite his illegal activities, Reina was also a family man, marrying Angelina Olivera and having nine children, five sons and four daughters. Throughout the early 1900s, Reina made a name for himself within the Morello gang, achieving the rank of captain and being charged with overseeing both the rank-and-file men and the operations of the organization.

In 1914, Reina and fellow mobster Jack Dragna were implicated in the murder of local poultry wholesaler Barnet Baff. The wealthy businessman "had been shot down in public by two Italian gunmen," with Reina and Dragna being suspects (Bush, 2015). Baff's murder had been orchestrated by his rivals in the poultry industry "after attempted mediation between Barnet and his poultry industry rivals came to naught" (Bush, 2015). Subsequently, said rivals hired organized crime members to dispatch Baff. Despite being a suspect, Reina was never seriously investigated for the shooting and later was dropped as a person of interest in the case. Around the outbreak of World War I and during the chaotic period within the ranks of the Morello gang, Reina broke away to form his own crime organization. This new organization, under Reina, began making a name for themselves in the criminal underworld of New York City, with the organization "[holding] a monopoly over the ice box distribution in the Bronx" ("Gaetano Reina," 2020).

The outbreak of the aforementioned Mafia-Camorra War did little to slow the expansion of the organization, with Reina staying well clear of the conflict, focusing heavily on solidifying his power throughout New York City neighborhoods such as the Bronx and East Harlem.

By the early 1920s, Reina had become a powerful crime boss and, along with his underboss Tommy Gagliano, had laid the foundations for what would become the Lucchese crime family. On the horizon, however, was a conflict that would drastically change the leadership of the proto-Lucchese crime family, as well as the structure of the American Mafia as a whole.

\

The Castellammarese War

When Reina split off from the destabilized Morello gang to form his own organization, two other prominent members did the same: Salvatore D'Aquila and Guiseppe "Joe the Boss" Masseria. By the late 1920s, Masseria had become extremely powerful and, after crushing D'Aquila and his rival organization when he attempted to seize power (mentioned briefly in the previous section), had absorbed the severely weakened Morello gang into his own organization, therefore becoming the *de facto* boss of the Morello gang. Reina, sensing the opportunity to cement and consolidate his own crime family's power, allied himself with Masseria. However, the profitable operations of the American Mafia were beginning to attract attention from overseas.

Vito Ferro, a prominent and powerful member of the Sicilian Mafia, decided to make a play for control of organized crime operations in the United States. From his base in Castellammare del Golfo, Sicily, Ferro sent Salvatore Maranzano to New York City, where Maranzano began attempting to seize control of the criminal enterprise operating there. Maranzano took control of what would later become known as the Bonanno crime family (known then as the Castellammarese family), and his positioning within the criminal underworld of New York City put him in direct conflict with Masseria and, by association, Reina.

The Castellammarese War lasted for just over a year, from February 1930 to April of the following year. There had been examples of conflict between the two factions prior to the official outbreak of the war, such as small firefights on the streets of New York City and the highjacking of each other's alcohol trucks (Prohibition in the

United States was in full swing at this time). Sensing that a large, open conflict between the two factions was inevitable, both Masseria and Maranzano began rallying support and swelling their ranks ahead of the oncoming battle for dominance. By 1929, "Masseria had developed a strong rivalry with the Castellammarese family headed by Maranzano," and tensions were at boiling point. The shot fired (if one will forgive the pun) that officially began the Castellammarese War was the murder of an individual that readers of this exploration will find wholly familiar: Gaetano Reina. However, before we delve into the crime boss' death, we must first backtrack slightly to discover how and why Reina's murder was ordered, as well as the events that it set in motion.

A Switch of Allegiance

Reina's criminal enterprises had been benefitting immensely from his alliance with Masseria. When Maranzano took control of the Castellamarese family and began applying pressure to Masseria, however, Reina's situation took a turn for the worse. In early 1930, Masseria demanded that Reina give him a cut of his organization's illicit gains. Reina quickly began considering an alliance with Maranzano, presumably to avoid this tribute to Masseria and build a more beneficial situation for himself and his organization. Masseria quickly learned of Reina's possible betrayal and, along with a young Charles "Lucky" Luciano and Reina's own underboss Tommy Gagliano, began plotting his murder. On February 26th, 1930, Reina exited an apartment on Sheridan Avenue in the Bronx. Some sources claim that the apartment was owned by his mistress Marie Ennis, while others claim "he was leaving his aunt's apartment after dinner" ("Gaetano Reina," 2020). Regardless of the purpose of Reina's visit to Sheridan Avenue, he was ambushed on the steps of the building, where "he was shot in the head with a double-barrelled shotgun, instantly killing him" ("Gaetano Reina," 2020). While it is clear who orchestrated the hit (that being Masseria, Luciano, and Gagliano), the identity of the gunman is contested. Many sources agree that it was Vito Genovese who pulled the trigger on Reina, although Joseph "Fat Joe" Pinzolo is another suspect.

A *New York Times* article published not long after the murder reported that Reina had been "shot and killed by one of two unidentified men," so it seems reasonable to suggest that both suspects were present at the scene (The New York Times, 1930). The article ran with the headline "Wealthy Ice Dealer Slain in Doorway" (The New York Times, 1930). Law enforcement had little luck in investigating Reina's murder, finding on his body only a firearm and a substantial amount of paper money, and failed to make an official arrest. Reina's murder acted as the catalyst for the start of the Castellammarese War, as well as a power struggle for the leadership of the Lucchese crime family.

With Reina out of the picture, his former underboss Gagliano was expecting to take his place. While the decision on who would succeed Reina fell to Masseria, Gagliano arguably assumed that, due to his assistance in orchestrating his former Boss' demise, he would be first choice. To his ire, Masseria bypassed Gagliano in favor of his own loyalist Joseph "Fat Joe" Pinzolo.

Pinzolo had already made a name for himself in the criminal underworld of New York City. In 1908, Pinzolo attempted to bomb a local business as part of an extortion scheme, for which he was arrested. To gain a lesser sentence, he ratted on his boss and was released mere years later. Gagliano, along with Lucchese crime family member Tommy Lucchese, were extremely frustrated at this turn of events, believing that "Pinzolo had been promoted in order to secure the underworld interests of Masseria and not the former Reina followers" ("Joseph Pinzolo," 2023). Pinzolo did little to help this tension, with him being "a most disagreeable man" and "the majority of his subordinates apparently [growing] to hate him with little time and effort" ("Joseph Pinzolo," 2023).

To truly encapsulate how Pinzolo was viewed by his contemporaries, one only needs to look at a quote made by Charles "Lucky" Luciano, who stated, "As big a shit as Masseria was, he didn't hold a candle to Pinzolo. That guy was fatter, uglier, and dirtier than Masseria was on the worst day when the old bastard didn't take a bath, which was most of the time" ("Joseph Pinzolo," 2023). Gagliano and Lucchese, along with another key member of the family called Dominick Petrilli, began planning to overthrow Pinzolo, "[forming] a splinter group within the family" ("Joseph Pinzolo," 2023).

In September 1930, the group put their plan into action, fueled by "their festering resentment and personal distaste [of Pinzolo]" and using "the general lawlessness unleashed by the Castellammarese War" as cover ("Joseph Pinzolo," 2023). Lured to a Manhattan office building leased by Tommy Lucchese, Pinzolo was shot and killed, ending his short-lived reign as Boss of the Lucchese crime family. As with the assassination of Reina, the shooter's identity is shrouded in doubt, with possible suspects including Petrilli, Girolamo Santucci, and even Lucchese himself. Pinzolo's death allowed Gagliano to take the mantle of Boss, with Lucchese as his second-in-command.

Gagliano, through his own plotting and violence, had made it to the top of the Lucchese crime family, but the Castellammarese War was still ongoing. However, this conflict was about to come to an abrupt end when, in 1931, Masseria himself was assassinated. In the lead-up to his death, Masseria's reputation was heavily waning. It is speculated that Gagliano and Lucchese had, much like their former Boss Gaetano Reina, covertly defected to Maranzano's faction not long after Pinzolo's installation as Boss, which the pair saw as a betrayal on Masseria's part. Their eventual murder of Pinzolo supports this theory, supporting the idea that "the Gagliano-Lucchese faction kept their alliance with the Maranzano forces even after the death of Reina while top family members acted as [spies] for the Maranzano faction by faking support for Masseria'" ("Joseph Pinzolo," 2023). Charles "Lucky" Luciano had also been "negotiating in secret with Maranzano," with the plan to ultimately end with the "[removal of] Masseria [to] install Luciano in place as head of the Mafia under Maranzano's faction" (Faddah, 2020). In April 1931, Masseria met with Luciano for lunch at a restaurant in Coney Island. After Luciano excused himself from the table, "four triggermen entered the restaurant and shot Masseria in the back at least five times" (Faddah, 2020). With that came the effective end of the Castellammarese War. However, "Masseria's death put an end to the war, but it did not put an end to the story" (Faddah, 2020).

CHAPTER 2
TROUBLE DOUBLED: THE TWO TOMMIES

In the aftermath of its chaotic, shifting, and violent 30-year period of infancy, the Lucchese crime family entered a state of relative stability. With Gagliano as Boss and Tommy Lucchese as his second-in-command, the organization consolidated its power and continued the expansion of its criminal enterprise throughout New York state and the wider United States. This is not to say that the American Mafia as a whole shared in this stability. On the contrary, the era that followed the Castellammarese War was one of drastic change, with the American Mafia, and by proxy, the Lucchese crime family, experiencing a massive restructuring that bore the shape and nature of the criminal syndicate that still exists today. In this chapter, we will explore the formation of the Five Families of New York, the overthrowing of a power-hungry Maranzano, the reign of Tommy Gagliano, and the passing of the torch to his successor Tommy Lucchese.

Formation of the Five Families

After his victory over Masseria in the Castellammarese War, Maranzano "had no one to stand in his way" (Faddah, 2020). He invited the bosses of every criminal organization across the United

States to New York City, where he held a summit at a hotel in Wappingers Falls. It was here that Maranzano laid out his vision for the future of the American Mafia. Framed as a peace plan, the new structure consisted of 24 organizations (or families) that were, in at least some senses, autonomous, as they were allowed to elect their own leadership. The hierarchy of each family was also clearly laid out as follows: Boss, underboss, *consigliere*, *capos*, soldiers, and associates. Nationwide, these families would be limited to one per city in an attempt to avoid unnecessary competition and consolidate the power of the overall American Mafia. The families of New York were organized differently due to the immense size and influence of organized crime in the state. Thus, the Five Families of New York were brought into existence: the Genovese family, the Colombo family, the Bonanno family, the Gambino family, and the Lucchese family. These families were headed by Charles "Lucky" Luciano, Joseph Profaci, Maranzano himself, Frank Scalice, and Tommy Gagliano, respectively. Although this reshuffling of the American Mafia's structure and leadership set out by Maranzano evidently laid the foundations for the modern American Mafia that operates to this day, Maranzano's aims were much more self-serving than simply the greater prosperity of the American Mafia as a whole. At the aforementioned meeting at Wappingers Falls, Maranzano made sure that he "asserted dominance over not only New York City but… over all other bosses [also]," installing himself as *capo di tutti capi*, translated into English as boss of all bosses (Faddah, 2020).

As one can probably imagine, Maranzano's self-appointment as *capo di tutti capi* was received poorly by other high-ranking American Mafia members and was seen as a self-interested and egotistical move. Maranzano wasted no time in further rubbing his perceived subordinates up the wrong way, stretching the muscles of his new-found power in a myriad of ways. Seemingly unaware of his fellow crime bosses' instant distaste with his title, or indeed believing he was now untouchable and therefore not caring, Maranzano began minimizing and cutting up the other crime families' rackets and taking them for himself. His arrogance was not exclusive to creating titles for himself either, spilling over into his treatment of others, regardless of their rank and reputation. It truly seems that Maranzano saw himself as invulnerable, and he frequently compared his organization to that of the Roman Empire. In Maranzano's own analogy, that would make him Julius Caesar. Comparing oneself to a tyrannical dictator, as well as building one's organization to resemble said dictator's chain of command, is a bold statement, to say the least.

Maranzano's antics quickly began to grate on the other crime bosses, most especially Charles "Lucky" Luciano. Despite being the heads of opposing factions during the Castellammarese War, both Maranzano and Masseria were considered to be "Mustache Petes." This term encapsulated the criminal philosophy of "old world Sicilian bosses who did things very traditionally" (Faddah, 2020). Individuals who followed this way of conducting criminal business were usually born in Italy (more specifically Sicily), "often refused to do business with non-Italians," and "looked down on non-Sicilian members of their own organizations" (Faddah, 2020). Luciano and his allies (including Lucchese family underboss Tommy Lucchese), on the other hand, had no such prejudice, having "largely grown up in America and saw these old world ways as unnecessary and stifling their potential for growth" (Faddah,

2020). Luciano's faction comprised the new generation of mafia members, with many referencing the group as 'The Young Turks" after the early 20th-century political reform movement that rebelled against the Ottoman Empire's absolute monarchy. Luciano and his faction had been maneuvering themselves politically since the Castellammarese War, with Luciano believing that neither Masseria nor Maranzano was fit to shape the future of the American Mafia. Knowing that "both bosses needed to be taken out" but not wanting to fight a war on two fronts, Luciano allied himself with Maranzano during the conflict, noticing that "Maranzano was looking likely at winning the Castellammarese War'" ("How Did Salvatore Maranzano Get Killed? - Death Photos," 2023). After Masseria's defeat, and seeing that the power "had… gone to his [Maranzano] head," Luciano and his faction set their sights on Maranzano, and their orders were shoot to kill.

Unseating the Capo Di Tutti Capi

Mere months after his victory in the Castellammarese War, Maranzano had painted a large target on his own back. Not being completely unaware of the tensions surrounding him, however, Maranzano had noticed that Luciano was getting too ambitious for his liking. Having been a conspirator in the assassination of his rival Masseria along with Luciano, Maranzano most likely thought that he might indeed be the one betrayed next. Hiring Irish gangster Vincent "Mad Dog" Coll to assassinate Luciano, Maranzano washed his hands of the matter, believing it to have been dealt with.

However, Luciano's influence permeated deeper than Maranzano had anticipated, as his own lieutenant Tommy Lucchese warned Luciano of the assassination plans. This was further compounded when, in September 1931, Maranzano ordered Luciano to his office in Manhattan. Thinking that this was a trap to murder him, Luciano acted quickly in order to strike first. Knowing that, due to ongoing tax issues, Maranzano was expecting an audit visit from federal government agents, Luciano sent four hitmen in disguise to deal with Maranzano. Said to consist of Vito Genovese, Albert Anastasia, Joe Adonis, and Samuel Levine, the hitmen entered Maranzano's office building posing as the expected tax men. Surprising the guards (one of whom was the would-be assassin of Luciano Vincent Coll), the hitmen disarmed them, entering Maranzano's office unopposed. The assassination of Maranzano was both gruesome and extremely violent. In some ways, the method of his murder represents the sheer hatred and distaste that Luciano and his faction had for him. Grabbing Maranzano and pinning him to a wall, the four hitmen "proceeded to stab him four times in the chest, stomach, and face (slicing his mouth) and then strangling him" before finishing him off (although it is not known whether Maranzano was already dead at this point) by "[firing] six shots at him from close range" ("How Did Salvatore Maranzano Get Killed? - Death Photos," 2023).

At the very least, Maranzano shared at least one aspect of his life with his idol Julius Caesar: the manner of his death. Interestingly enough, the only confirmed photographs of Maranzano are those taken at the crime scene of his assassination. The images are gruesome and easily accessed with a cursory internet search. If one can stomach it, one can view the final image of the man who wanted to be emperor of the American Mafia: Salvatore Maranzano.

With Maranzano dead, Luciano and his faction of young mobsters were poised to pave the direction of the newly-organized American Mafia. Luciano, recognizing that organized crime in the United States was still in dire need of restructuring, chose to maintain the general shape set out by Maranzano. He did, however, do away with the title of *capo di tutti capi*, believing it to only cause conflict between families and be a title that would make him a target for other ambitious competitors.

Not long after the death of Maranzano, Luciano called a meeting of the crime organization bosses nationwide. Here, he set out what he thought should replace the *capo di tutti capi*: the Mafia Commission. Luciano saw the Mafia Commission taking a multitude of roles: "making money in joint ventures with other families, resolving disputes between families, formally recognizing new Bosses" as well as "taking steps to maintain order between families including the use of murder" (Petepiece, 2018).

Indeed, Luciano was keen to leave the bloody civil wars and destructive gang disputes of the 1920s in the past and wanted to consolidate the power of all criminal organizations into a central body in order to protect the interests of wider criminal enterprise in the United States. This new Mafia Commission would be made up of a "board of directors" who would oversee criminal operations in the United States as well as serve as mediators if any disputes arose between families. On the board would sit each Boss of the Five Families of New York, in addition to Chicago Outfit Boss Al Capone and Buffalo crime family Boss Stefano Maggadino.

As we continue to see time and time again when delving into the history of the American Mafia, Luciano was not creating the Mafia

Commission just for the benefit of criminal enterprise as a whole but was also positioning himself at the head of it. The board needed a chairman, and, of course, Luciano installed himself as that chairman, effectively placing himself in charge of all criminal activities in the United States. His plan was, in some respects, a mirror of Maranzano's, who had been killed for it. However, Luciano was more tactical, planning on subtly maintaining a stranglehold over all the other families and, by association, criminal enterprise as a whole. The other crime bosses approved of the idea, and the creation of the Mafia Commission was realized, lasting long after the deaths of its original board members and through to the modern day.

Now we have covered the events that ended the Castellammarese War and led to both the restructuring of the American Mafia and the creation of the Mafia Commission; it is now prevalent to put this into the context of the Lucchese crime family.

Tommy Gagliano

Hailing from Corleone, Sicily, a town "famous for its mafioso," Tommy Gagliano came to the United States in 1905 when he was around 22 years of age (Dickson, 2013). Arriving in New York City, Gagliano quickly married fellow Sicilian Giuseppina Pomilla. From this marriage, he gained a brother-in-law in the form of a man named Nunzio Pomilla, and the two set up a hoisting and lathing business in the Bronx. The legality of this business venture was ropey, however, as it was used as a front for the pair to "[begin] working for the family headed by Bronx-based gangster Gaetano Reina" (Dickson, 2013). There are some suggestions amongst sources that indicate Gagliano entering the criminal underworld of

New York City much earlier, with reports that he "joined... as an associate of the crime family then headed by Giuseppe 'The Clutch Hand' Morello," which readers of this exploration know to be the leader of the Morello gang at this time (Dickson, 2013). However, these suggestions are not widely substantiated, but it is clear that Gagliano joined Reina's gang when he and Pomilla moved their operation into the Bronx. Gagliano rapidly ascended the ranks of Reina's proto-Lucchese crime family. Reina, like Gagliano, was from Corleone and was of a similar age, leading to a common ground for the two to bond over and assuring Gagliano's prompt rise through the ranks. Gagliano became Reina's underboss around 1922 and ranked amongst the most powerful members of Reina's organization, along with the likes of Tommy Lucchese and Stefano Rondelli.

As previously covered, by the late 1920s, "the entire New York mob was either at war or on the verge of it" (Dickson, 2013). When Reina attempted to defect to Salvatore Maranzano before the beginning of the Castellammarese War, Gagliano conspired with rival faction leader Joseph Masseria to assassinate Reina. The hit was successful and Gagliano expected to be promoted to Reina's former position. When Masseria instead installed Joseph Pinzolo as Boss, Gagliano pulled a double betrayal and joined Maranzano's faction. When the war ended with Masseria's killing, Maranzano restructured the American Mafia and formed the Five Families of New York, one of which Gagliano presided over as Boss. After Charles "Lucky" Luciano's rebellion and Maranzano's murder, Gagliano retained his leadership over the Lucchese crime family, as well as gaining a seat on the board of the Mafia Commission. This was the state of affairs for Gagliano in 1931, and after appointing Tommy Lucchese as his underboss, he began to run his organization from the shadows.

Unlike what one would expect from a Boss of a Mafia crime family, Gagliano always kept a low profile throughout his leadership, and very little is known about his life during this period. The only charge that was ever brought against him by law enforcement during his tenure as Boss seems to be a conviction for tax evasion in 1932, for which he served 15 months in prison. Known as "The Quiet Don," Gagliano preferred to speak his orders through the mouthpiece of his underboss Tommy Lucchese, who became the public face of Gagliano's Lucchese crime family. Under Gagliano, the organization furthered its own interests and expanded its enterprise in industries such as the black market sugar trade and gasoline rationing. This style of leadership served both the Lucchese crime family in general and Gagliano personally, as he sat on the ruling panel of the Commission during its developmental early period and managed to avoid the majority of its teething issues.

In 1936, Luciano was arrested and sentenced to prison and later deported back to Italy. With the absence of their most powerful member, other individuals on the Commission began maneuvering for power. In the end, the Commission fell into the hands of an alliance of Bosses: Vincent Manango, Joe Bonanno, Stefano Maggadino, and Joe Profaci. Gagliano steered his organization carefully through this period of struggle, staying well clear of any personal political maneuvering and making sure not to step on the toes of this new alliance within the Commission. This strategy worked and was "a rather remarkable achievement considering the allegiances, counter-allegiances, enmities, and backstabbing that marked the early Commission" (Dickson, 2013). As if to hammer home his preferred philosophy, Gagliano was even secretive in death, with no one concretely knowing when exactly he died. Tommy Lucchese, his successor as Boss, was quoted saying that Gagliano died in 1951. However, a theory posits that Gagliano stepped down in 1951 and handed power over to Lucchese with the arrangement being kept secret in order to keep law enforcement off the scent. The theory suggests that, after two years of anonymity, Gagliano died in 1953, which is the year many historians and academics favor when discussing his death date. His cause of death is listed as natural causes. Regardless of the exact date of Gagliano's death, his underboss Tommy Luchesse, took his place in 1951. To truly encapsulate the uniqueness of this early Lucchese crime family Boss, writer Mike Dickson (2013) states, "Gagliano is remembered today (when he's remembered at all) as a faceless boss from the early years, but that may be his greatest achievement."

CHAPTER 3

POWER AND PROFIT: THE LUCCHESE ERA

At the turn of the 1950s, Tommy Lucchese took over as Boss of the Lucchese crime family from "The Quiet Don" Tommy Gagliano. The *de facto* street boss and public face of the organization long before his ascension to the top of the pile, Lucchese spent "14 years as actual boss [and] 22 years as underboss" of the Lucchese crime family (Cipollini, 2017). It seems reasonable to state that Lucchese left "his permanent stamp" on the organization, especially considering that the family kept his namesake as their own from his installation as Boss to the modern day (Dickson, 2013). Lucchese steered the organization through the 1950s and half of the 1960s, creating new opportunities and cementing power over the already existing criminal operations run by the Lucchese crime family. In this chapter, we will explore the early life of Tommy Lucchese, his ascension and tenure as Boss of the family, and his close ties with fellow Five Families member organization, the Gambino crime family.

The Lucchese Namesake

Tommy Lucchese (birthname Gaetano) was born in Palermo, Sicily, in 1899 to parents Baldasserre and Francesca Lucchese. The surname "Lucchese" suggests "family origins from the Sicilian city of Lucca Sicula" (Harlem World Magazine, 2023).

Like many of his predecessors, Lucchese and his family immigrated to the United States, arriving in New York City in 1911. The family settled in New York's East Harlem neighborhood, which at the time was a predominantly Italian section of the city. This area must have suited the Luccheses well as, when they moved out of their first apartment at 213 East 106th Street, they remained in the neighborhood, traveling only a few streets away to 316 East 118th Street. Lucchese's father, Baldasserre, made his living hauling cement, and Lucchese also found a job in manual labor; as a teenager, he was employed in a factory that manufactured munitions. He kept this job until 1919, when Lucchese lost the forefinger and thumb of his right hand in a workplace accident. It was this accident that earned him a nickname, "Three Finger Brown," although nobody was brave enough to refer to him by this moniker "except for the cop that labeled him and the press that kept the [nickname] alive for years" (Cipollini, 2017). The police officer that first gave the nickname did so in 1920 when Lucchese was arrested on auto theft charges. While he was being booked, said police officer "compared Lucchese's deformed hand with that of Mordecai 'Three Finger' Brown, a popular Major League baseball player" of the time (Harlem World Magazine, 2023). The nickname stuck despite it being an alias that Lucchese always disliked. Interestingly, this arrest (and later conviction in 1921) was the only time that Lucchese ever spent in prison and, even then, he only served a little more than a year for the crime ("Tommy Lucchese," 2023).

Lucchese had been involved with the illegal side of New York City long before his arrest in 1920, however. When Lucchese was in his 20's, "he joined forces with fellow future Mob dignitary Charles

'Lucky' Luciano" 'as part of the 107th Street Gang ("Tommy Lucchese," 2023). His main front was that of a window-washing business, where those who "refused to buy window washing would have their windows broken" (Harlem World Magazine, 2023). Lucchese and Luciano, as part of the 107th Street Gang, were "working under the protection and auspices of Prohibition-era Mafia lord [Gaetano] Reina," running criminal activities such as burglarizing stores and stealing wallets on the streets of New York City ("Tommy Lucchese," 2023). His arrest in 1920 marked the first of only six throughout his entire criminal career. He was arrested in 1927 under suspicion of receiving stolen goods and again in 1928 for the murder of Louis Cerasuolo, although he was convicted for neither. Leaving his 1921 conviction for auto theft the only time he ever spent in prison, he was released back into the world in 1923. By then, something was bubbling up in the criminal underworld of the United States that Lucchese was about to become a key player in.

Author and crime historian Christian Cipollini (2017) writes that "Lucchese played a prominent role… during and after the so-called Castellammarese War… and helped reshape the underworld landscape." With this, Cipollini hits the nail directly on the head, so to speak, as it is abundantly clear that Lucchese had a hand in the major events of the late 1920s and early 1930s that drastically altered the criminal underworld of the United States. At the close of the Castellammarese War in 1931, when Salvatore Maranzano altered the structure of organized crime in New York by creating the Five Families, Tommy Gagliano took command of the Lucchese crime family and Tommy Lucchese "slid into the No. 2 seat and loyally served as Gagliano's underboss for the ensuing two decades'" (The Mob Museum, 2023). When tensions arose between

Maranzano and Luciano, Lucchese was the one that "alerted Luciano that he was marked for death," allowing Luciano time to orchestrate Maranzano's own assassination (Harlem World Magazine, 2023).

After Mafia Commission chairman Luciano was imprisoned in 1936, and an alliance of mob bosses was formed to take control of the Commission, Lucchese was, for all intents and purposes, the public leader of the Lucchese crime family, making sure that the organization continued to prosper in such dangerous times. Being underboss to "The Quiet Don" put Lucchese in a unique position. Preferring to stay in the shadows and out of the public eye, Gagliano spoke his orders through Lucchese, with him even "[attending] the mob Havana conference in Cuba as Gagliano's representative" in 1943 (Harlem World Magazine, 2023). When Gagliano died, Lucchese succeeded him and "the crime family assumed his name" (Cipollini, 2017). Now in charge, Lucchese wasted no time in building on what his predecessor left for him.

Political Maneuvers

Despite the date of Gagliano's death being shrouded in mystery, Lucchese took the reins of the Lucchese crime family in 1951, appointing Stefano LaSalle as his underboss and Vincenzo Rao as his *consigliere*. Lucchese mobilized the organization, taking on many of Gagliano's methods of leadership while also expanding and morphing with the times. Lucchese used "brains as much as, if not more than, brawn to establish himself as one of the elite figures in America's Mafia history" (Cipollina, 2017).

Under Lucchese, the Lucchese crime family created and maintained a stranglehold in the trucking industry by gaining control of key unions and trade associations, such as local Teamsters unions and workers' cooperatives (Harlem World Magazine, 2023). The real uniqueness and brilliance of Lucchese's tenure as Boss, however, was the importance he placed on connections. Lucchese, being a "politically connected godfather," built and nurtured close relationships with many prominent New York politicians (The Mob Museum, 2023). These powerful individuals included members of the judiciary as well as two New York City mayors: William O'Dwyer and Vincent Impellitteri, the latter of which allegedly owed his rise in politics to Lucchese. Having those in positions of political power as allies afforded Lucchese and his crime family breathing space when operating their criminal rackets.

Lucchese also made sure to maintain relations with other crime bosses, such as the Tampa Mafia's Santo Trafficante Jr. The pair operated and oversaw an extensive narcotics trafficking enterprise, and Trafficante Jr. saw Lucchese as somewhat of a mentor. Lucchese and Trafficante Jr.'s father had kept a longtime alliance between them during the 1940s and Lucchese had assisted in the training of Trafficante Jr. in mafia traditions. This relationship blossomed into a lucrative criminal business for both crime bosses, and the pair would be frequently seen having dinner together in New York City. All of these beneficial and powerful connections made Lucchese "one of the most well-respected [crime] bosses of the Post-war era" (Harlem World Magazine, 2023).

Although, as a crime boss, Lucchese was adamant in keeping a low profile, making sure his criminal enterprises continued to be profitable, and accumulating considerable respect in the shadows away from the prying eyes of the press, he would "begin seeing his name regularly printed in newspapers by 1952", due to "enhanced law enforcement scrutiny and public interest in underworld intrigue" (Cipollini, 2017). Indeed, despite Lucchese's remarkable ability to keep himself out of prison, this did not mean that law enforcement did not have him on their radar. In fact, "federal authorities had been investigating Lucchese since 1943," as this was the year that his naturalization application was finally approved (Cipollini, 2017). For the sake of context, naturalization is a legal process in which an individual can gain citizenship in a country that they are not originally from. This can occur due to various factors but, in Lucchese's case, was accepted due to his prolonged residency in the United States.

Still, this official application put Lucchese directly in the spotlight of law enforcement, although they were unable to locate Lucchese until 1952, a year into his reign as Boss. Law enforcement had collared Lucchese due to false statements made on his naturalization application but got more than they bargained for when they pulled him in for questioning. Lucchese was put in front of a private committee that proceeded to question him about the activities of both the Lucchese crime family and the American Mafia as a whole, although Lucchese remained "generally cryptic or entirely tight-lipped… during questioning" (Cipollini, 2017). Despite Lucchese's less-than-cooperative demeanor, law enforcement were able to coerce a limited amount of useful information regarding Lucchese's criminal operations in narcotics and his ties to powerful politicians. These revelations fueled U.S. attorney general James P. McGranery's campaign to have Lucchese deported. McGranery's wish to see Lucchese deported never came to pass, however, as, in 1958, "the Supreme Court dismissed the denaturalization charges against Lucchese" (Cipollini, 2017).

As they say, hindsight sees perfectly, and it is arguably clear to anyone looking through a historical lens at Lucchese and his reign that he was most definitely involved in organized crime, which would be putting it mildly. However, Lucchese was extremely adept in masking his criminal activities behind a front as a well-to-do and successful businessman. Lucchese's facade as a "low-key, successful garment district entrepreneur" had been a persona he had been crafting since the 1930s (Cipollini, 2017). In reality, Lucchese "[ruled] over the textile trade with an iron fist," frequently using feared hit squad Murder, Inc., led by Louis "Lepke" Buchalter, as his muscle to "place a vise grip on the industry" (The Mob Museum, 2023).

Lucchese's illusion of legitimacy was so effective, in fact, that "the reality of Lucchese's criminal life was an alarming revelation for a number of prominent, legitimate friends and associates who, before the government inquiries, had little idea of the true background of the man they thought… was an upstanding businessman" (Cipollina, 2017). Despite the large amount of attention from the government and law enforcement, it did little to damage either Lucchese's social standing or criminal enterprises. Either to keep up appearances or to rub salt in the wounds of frustrated law enforcement (or perhaps both), Lucchese continuously denied all knowledge of the American Mafia or the criminal underworld. Publicly, Lucchese stated, "I make $100,00 a year with my dress factories. I got 1,500 people working for me. I give them all the fringe benefits, plus turkeys, twice a year. If a girl has a baby, I give her a carriage or $50. If it's twins, the parents get a car. Triplets, I build them a house. But nobody's had twins or triplets yet" (Cipollini, 2017). This tongue-in-cheek statement assumedly drew the ire of those out to arrest Lucchese and perfectly encapsulates the intelligent and practical manner in which he approached his criminal profession.

The Lucchese-Gambino Alliance

As we have seen, Lucchese was a man who put great importance on his ties and connections with other prominent individuals. It is clear that this philosophy benefitted him greatly, but there was one particular connection that Lucchese nurtured that trumped all others when it came to the power and influence it garnered: that of Carlo Gambino of the Gambino crime family.

When Lucchese gained leadership over the Lucchese crime family, he formed an alliance with both Gambino and Vito Genovese, vowing to help them climb to the top of their own respective crime families. This alliance was beneficial to Lucchese as, after Gambino and Genovese took control of their organizations, the trio would make a play for control of the Mafia Commission and, by proxy, take ownership over the majority of organized crime enterprises across the United States. Frank Costello, the Boss of the Genovese crime family (then the Luciano crime family), was first on the list. In May of 1957, Costello was shot outside of his apartment building by gunman Vincent Gigante under orders from Genovese, Lucchese, and Gambino. Although Costello survived, he was "shaken by the assassination attempt, [and] soon retired" (Harlem World Magazine, 2023). A doorman of the apartment building did identified the shooter as Gigante, but, perhaps out of fear, Costello testified that this was not the case as he did not recognize his assassin. With this, Genovese quickly took control of the Genovese crime family.

Then, the alliance turned their crosshairs toward Albert Anastasia, the Boss of the Gambino crime family (then the Mangano crime family). In the barbershop of the Park Sheraton Hotel in Manhattan, Anastasia arrived for a scheduled appointment. Strangely, Anastasia's driver left to take a walk, leaving Anastasia unprotected. As he settled into the barber's chair, two men rushed into the shop and opened fire on Anastasia. It is rumored that, after the first round of bullets were fired at him, Anastasia lunged forward to combat his assailants. However, in the confusion and shock, Anastasia had actually attacked the reflections of the gunmen in the barbershop mirror. The two assassins continued their assault, shooting Anastasia dead. The main suspects in the shooting were the Gallo brothers, who were members of the Colombo crime family, and the hole at the top of the Mangano crime family was quickly filled by Gambino.

In the aftermath of these two high-profile assassinations, Lucchese, Gambino, and Genovese were now in control of three of the five New York families. They held a considerable amount of influence on the Mafia Commission. However, as many who have a knowledge of the criminal underworld know, alliances are easily broken as personal interests shift.

In a situation of betrayal within betrayal, Lucchese and Gambino began to conspire against their former ally Genovese. The main catalyst for this decision came after the disastrous Apalachin meeting of 1957. After Genovese's rise to power, he reveled in his success and newfound influence. This, however, was seemingly not enough for Genovese, as he wanted the other mafia leaders to recognize this power. In an effort to legitimize his control over the Luciano crime family, Genovese called a meeting of the wider American Mafia, choosing the rural location of Apalachin, New York, as the meeting place, away from the prying eyes of law enforcement. Genovese's plan was not as inconspicuous as he had hoped. On the contrary, "the dozens of gleaming Cadillacs parked next to the only paved stretch of backroad" that led to the meeting place caught the attention of the New York State Police (Dunn, 2021). The meeting was raided and all in all, over 60 mobsters were arrested.

Lucchese managed to avoid arrest, but his *consigliere* Vincenzo Rao and Carlo Gambino himself were collared by law enforcement. This was a massive blow to the American Mafia and humiliated Genovese, as he saw his respect diminish amongst his fellow crime bosses. Lucchese and Gambino assisted in getting Genovese arrested and convicted on a narcotics charge, for which he was imprisoned in 1959. Although attempting to maintain some semblance of his power from behind bars, Genovese died of a heart attack 10 years later whilst still in prison.

By the beginning of the 1960s, the Lucchese-Gambino alliance was firmly in control of the Mafia Commission. They supported the Gallo brothers (who had carried out Anastasia's assassination under their orders) in their overthrow of the Profaci crime family Boss, Joe Profaci, seeing the opportunity to take over the family's criminal rackets. They also stamped out a rebellion against their stranglehold over the Mafia Commission.

In 1963, Joseph Magliocco and Bonanno crime family Boss Joseph Bonanno hatched an ambitious plan to murder Lucchese, Gambino, and other members of the Mafia Commission in order to take control. Magliocco contracted Joseph Colombo to carry out the assassinations, but Colombo did the opposite and reported the plan directly to the Mafia Commission. The reasons for Colombo's actions here are not clear, but it is reasonable to suggest that he either saw an opportunity to get on the good side of the Mafia Commission or feared retaliation if the plan failed. Regardless of Colombo's motives, Magliocco and Bonanno's plan failed spectacularly, as the Mafia Commission immediately summoned the pair to explain themselves. Through their investigation, it was evident that Bonanno was the true mastermind of the plot, and Bonanno immediately went into hiding in Montreal, Canada. Magliocco, on the other hand, "badly shaken" and in ill health, confessed to everything and was promptly forced into retirement (Harlem World Magazine, 2023).

The Lucchese-Gambino alliance stretched further than plotting coups and crushing rebellions. The "Gambino and Lucchese syndicates [shared] most of the vast and profitable set of rackets being run out of the Idlewild… airport" in New York City ("Tommy Lucchese," 2023). Lucchese and Gambino "exercised control over the airport management security and all airport unions," creating an extremely profitable enterprise for both crime bosses (Harlem World Magazine, 2023). The Lucchese crime family's exploits at the

Idlewild airport have been immortalized in the Martin Scorsese (1990) classic *Goodfellas*.

Part of the Idlewild airport rackets had been given to Gambino as a wedding gift as, in 1962, Lucchese's daughter married Gambino's son. In return, Gambino offered a $30,000 gift. With this marriage, the Lucchese-Gambino alliance was further strengthened, and the two families "now controlled the airport, the Commission, and most organized crime in New York City" (Harlem World Magazine, 2023). In the end, Tommy Lucchese died not from assassination or betrayal but from failing health. Suffering from multiple problems relating to his health in the preceding years, Lucchese died from a brain tumor at his home in 1967. During his reign as Boss of the Lucchese crime family, Lucchese had been "branded… a top criminal, if not the single most important of Mafia bosses at the time" (Cipollini, 2017). Indeed, there were so many attendees linked to the criminal underworld at his funeral that undercover law enforcement was present. At his death, Lucchese had left the Lucchese crime family in a position of great power, influence, and wealth. He had even chosen a successor to pass the torch to. However, this would prove more complicated than Lucchese could ever have imagined.

CHAPTER 4

INTERNATIONAL SMUGGLING: CARMINE "MR. GRIBBS" TRAMUNTI AND THE FRENCH CONNECTION

Throughout organized crime history, there have always been movements to adapt and monopolize on emerging criminal enterprises. As the world moved into the latter half of the 20th century, the acquisition, movement, and sale of narcotics began to take center stage and garnered the interest of organized crime in the United States. There were those, perhaps considered to be old-fashioned, mobsters that were against involvement in the narcotics trade due to the law enforcement attention it attracted, preferring to stick with the old-style Mafia activities such as racketeering and extortion. However, money talks, and considering the large payouts connected with the narcotics trade, more forward-thinking crime bosses began modernizing their organizations, involving themselves heavily with this emerging criminal enterprise. One such crime boss was Carmine "Mr. Gribbs" Tramunti. In this chapter, we will explore the rise of Tramunti through the ranks of the Lucchese crime family, the infamous French Connection operation, and its subsequent investigation, as well as the series of arrests and convictions that led to Tramunti's downfall.

Carmine Tramunti

Carmine "Mr. Gribbs" Tramunti was born in Naples, Italy, in 1910. When he was three years of age, his family traveled to the United States, where they found themselves settling in New York City's Harlem neighborhood. In 1922, Tramunti was enrolled in a Catholic reform school due to his repeated truancy from his previous school. In December of 1930, when Tramunti was 20 years old, "[he] accosted a rent collector in his neighborhood, robbing him of his collections" (Dickson, 2015). Whilst he was arrested for the assault and robbery, the judge that presided over his case dismissed the charges, citing a lack of evidence.

It is unclear as to whether Tramunti was connected with the American Mafia this early in his life, but this may be evidence for such a connection as it was "a norm for that time when someone was reluctant to take the witness stand against someone with ties to the mob" (Dickson, 2015).

The accosting of the rent collector seems to be Tramunti's first run-in with law enforcement, and he would go on to make a habit of it. In 1931, Tramunti was convicted on a felonious assault charge and sentenced to 6–15 years in prison. He served his sentence at the Sing Sing Correctional Facility, where, "after a brief release and subsequent incarceration for a parole violation," Tramunti was finally released in 1938 (Dickson, 2015). Falling immediately back into criminal activities, Tramunti took over operations of "one of the most lucrative craps games in New York called the Harlem Game (Dickson, 2015). Standing at five feet ten inches tall with a beefy frame, Tramunti was an imposing figure and his physicality assumedly served him well in his criminal career. Tramunti was married and had two children, living in the Queens borough of New York City. Tramunti experienced a personal tragedy around the late 1930s when one of his sons, Louis, died at the age of 14. It is around this time that it is thought that Tramunti "became embedded with the Lucchese crime family" (Dickson, 2015).

For the next three decades, Tramunti would rise through the ranks of the Lucchese crime family under both Tommy Gagliano and Tommy Lucchese. Tramunti owed much of this ascension within the family to his close ties with Carlo Gambino, "using his friendship and Gambino's power to climb the ladder within the Lucchese [crime family]" (Dickson, 2015). Gambino had already been nurturing a strong alliance with the Lucchese crime family, so it is no surprise that Tramunti benefitted from Gambino's support.

Then, in 1967, current Boss Tommy Lucchese died of a brain tumor and a successor needed to take his place. Tramunti had risen to the rank of *capo* by this time, but Lucchese had signaled to the Mafia Commission that his chosen successor should be respected *capo* Anthony "Tony Ducks" Corallo. However, Corallo was imprisoned when Lucchese died, and Lucchese's second choice Ettore Coco was also facing legal trouble. Coco did serve as acting Boss of the Lucchese crime family, albeit for a very short time, after which he returned to acting as a *capo*. Another candidate to succeed Lucchese was his *consigliere* Vincenzo Rao but, again, he was facing scrutiny from law enforcement.

Gambino, sensing an opportunity to have a close ally at the top of the Lucchese crime family, "pushed the Commission to have Tramunti succeed him [Lucchese] due to his business leadership and general intelligence" (Dickson, 2015). With this backing from the powerful Gambino, the Mafia Commission accepted Tramunti as the new Boss of the Lucchese crime family. There are suggestions that the Mafia Commission saw Tramunti as a compromise candidate for the position, acceptable across all of the different factions that made up the American Mafia. What is clear is that the Mafia Commission only gave Tramunti leadership over the Lucchese crime family under the stipulation that he would be replaced when first choice Anthony Corallo was released from prison and "were secure enough in their decision knowing Gambino was there to keep things together for the Lucchese [crime family]" (Dickson, 2015). After this short period of shifting candidates, Tramunti became the Boss of the Lucchese crime family in 1967. However, he would not come anywhere close to the respect and success of his predecessor, his relatively short tenure of 6 years as Boss being marred by almost constant arrests, convictions, and jail time. These continuous speed bumps in Tramunti's criminal career came to a head with his involvement in the infamous French Connection scheme and subsequent criminal trial.

The French Connection

Before we delve into the specifics of Tramunti's ties to and involvement with the French Connection operation, it seems prevalent to first explain the operation in a more general context. In short, the French Connection was an international drug trafficking operation where heroin was smuggled from Indochina across Turkey to France and then on to the United States and Canada, either directly or occasionally via Cuba. This expansive narcotics operation spanned from the 1930s to the 1970s and "would permanently disrupt the American Mafia, sparking a violent power struggle which lasted for decades'" (Plain Sight Productions, 2020).

The first evidence of the operation was found in France when heroin labs were discovered near Marseille in 1937. "Run by the Corsican Mafia... [the French Connection] was the main global network for the manufacture and trafficking of heroin," including the vast majority of the narcotic within the United States (Marchant, 2012). The name of the operation came from both its ties to France as well as much of the heroin entering the United States through French-speaking Canadian provinces such as Quebec.

The true scope of the French Connection was a global one, "far from being a single organization, it was a configuration born out of the meeting of different Corsican families and unscrupulous crooks who had their fingers in semi-private, semi-public structures in a worldwide, clandestine market" (Marchant, 2012). Of course, with an operation of this size, the details and factors are extremely complex. However, what is more specific in regard to this exploration is the French Connection's relevance to the American Mafia. Indeed, the sale of narcotics was a profitable one, and the American Mafia were completely aware of that. In a situation where narcotics were moving through their territory regardless, it only seemed practical to control it and reap the lucrative benefits. In fact, French drug dealers began exporting narcotics to the United States due to requests from the New York crime organizations. There were also cultural elements to this exchange that strengthened links between the heroin manufacturers and the American Mafia, as "Corsicans spoke Italian and had Mafia ethics in common"

(Marchant, 2012). When the narcotics then arrived in the United States, the merchandise was transferred to the American Mafia before being further divided between the numerous families nationwide.

Around the late 1960s and early 1970s, the French Connection had helped supply millions of dollars worth of heroin to the American Mafia. Seeing a large spike in the trade of the narcotic in the United States attracted the attention of law enforcement, and they attempted to move on those they suspected of running the operations within the United States. After cracking down on the trafficking and sale of the narcotic, including a bust in New York that saw officers uncovering 246 pounds of heroin in a small car that had traveled overseas on an ocean liner from France in 1968, the New York City Police Department had managed to collect approximately $70 million worth of heroin, which they kept in lock-up at the New York City Police's property office in Manhattan.

Enter Vincent Papa and Anthony Loria Sr., two members of the Lucchese crime family and known drug traffickers. Both men were known to federal agents and had acquired rap sheets with multiple drug-related offenses. Indeed, along with their gang, they were responsible for the distribution of nearly one million dollars worth of heroin across the East Coast of the United States. This achievement, however, was small fry in comparison to what they had planned next, with the two becoming known as "The Men Who Stole the French Connection." During the early 1970s, the pair managed to systematically steal the $70 million worth of heroin sitting in lock-up. How they executed this feat is still up for debate, and the discovery of the heist sparked a corruption investigation within the New York Police Department.

One theory is that corrupt police officers allowed Papa, Loria, and their associates into the lock-up, where the men were then free to plunder the seized heroin to their heart's content. Another posits that it was the corrupt police officers that did the plundering, having been paid off by the gang to do so. In order to cover their tracks, the gang replaced the bags of heroin with both bags of corn starch and flour, with officers only identifying the decoys when they noticed that insects had begun feasting on the "heroin." As impressive as this heist scheme was, neither Papa nor Loria got away with it, ultimately being arrested and charged along with a myriad of other criminal mobsters during the eventual deconstruction of the French Connection scheme. Both men were imprisoned, and Papa's end came when he was stabbed to death by a fellow inmate. Both law enforcement's unraveling of the international drug smuggling operation and the daring heist pulled by Papa and his gang are fictionalized in the films *The French Connection* (1971) and *French Connection II* (1975), directed by William Friedkin and John Frankenheimer, respectively, with the former winning five Academy Awards and being considered amongst the best movies ever made.

Trading Places

Tramaunti also found himself embroiled in the unmasking of the French Connection. However, this would serve as the finale to his tenure as Boss of the Lucchese crime family, as he faced the mercy of law enforcement multiple times before this. In 1970, Tramunti was "indicted on 14 counts of stock fraud for allegedly taking over an investment firm in Florida" (Dickson, 2015). Tramunti was accused of taking the Miami investment company by force, although a year later, in 1971, he was acquitted of the crime. It was not long before Tramunti again found himself in the spotlight of law enforcement as, later that year, he was indicted on criminal contempt charges for "lying to a grand jury about his contact with Lucchese *capo* Paul Vario" (Dickson, 2015). To note, Vario ran many lucrative criminal rackets and was serving as Tramunti's *consigliere* at the time. Tramunti could not dodge the strong arm of the law on this occasion and was sentenced to three years in prison in August of 1972.

It was whilst serving his time for criminal contempt that Tramunti received the conviction that would effectively end both his time as Boss of the Lucchese crime family and his criminal career as a whole. After law enforcement had uncovered the major heroin route coming into the United States from France (what readers of this exploration know as the French Connection), 44 mobsters in the United States were indicted on narcotics trafficking charges, Tramunti amongst them. The trial that followed was nicknamed after the smuggling operation and Tramunti was ultimately convicted, being named as "the financier of the French Connection" (Dickson, 2015). The smoking gun, so to speak, that ended Tramunti was when a former barista of a cafe testified that they had witnessed drug dealer Louis Inglese discuss a deal with Tramunti, with Tramunti nodding his head in agreement during the conversation. This testimony was all the prosecution needed to put him away, and Tramunti was convicted and sentenced to 15 years in federal prison in 1973. The judge that presided over the case described Tramunti as dangerous and, upon hearing his sentence, Tramunti stated, "I may be a mobster and may have done bad things but I am not a drug dealer" (Dickson, 2015).

Anthony Corallo, who had been first choice for Boss of the Lucchese crime family back in 1967, had been released from prison in 1970. Some historians believe that Corallo became Boss with immediate effect on his release, with the legally-troubled Tramunti merely acting as a "front" boss for the next three years. Regardless, with Tramunti behind bars, Corallo quickly filled the gap at the top of the Lucchese crime family. With his imprisonment, Tramunti would never see the outside of a cell again as, in 1978, he "died of natural causes while still serving his sentence" (Dickson, 2015).

CHAPTER 5

"TONY DUCKS": THE REIGN OF ANTHONY CORALLO

During the mid-1970s, the Lucchese crime family was still in a very powerful position. Having just had a Boss that attracted conviction after conviction from law enforcement did little to stem the tide, and the organization still retained the influence, wealth, and respect it had built up during Tommy Lucchese's era. When Corallo officially took leadership in 1973, the landscape of his family, and indeed organized crime in general, was still well and truly in his favor. However, Corallo's reign would hit one too many snags, ending in a trial that would shake the very foundations of the American Mafia's structure and hierarchy. In this chapter, we will explore the early life of Anthony Corallo, the state of the Lucchese crime family under his leadership, a costly mistake on Corallo's part that invited the Federal Bureau of Investigation right into the heart of organized crime, and a criminal proceeding that aimed to cut off the head of the American Mafia.

Anthony Corallo

Anthony Corallo was born in New York City in February 1913, giving him the accolade of the first Lucchese crime Boss to be born in the United States. Raised in East Harlem, Corallo "worked, at least for a while, as a tile-setter" (Feuer, 2000). It was not long into Corallo's life, however, that he began dabbling in the criminal underworld of New York City.

As early as the 1920s, Corallo had joined the 107th Street Gang, who operated in East Harlem, an early criminal organization where future mob bosses Charles "Lucky" Luciano and Tommy Lucchese cut their teeth. 1929 saw Corallo's first arrest at the tender age of 16 years old. He was accused of grand larceny (or theft in layman's terms) but was never convicted. By 1935, Corallo was a member of the Lucchese crime family under Tommy Gagliano. It had been Gagliano's underboss Tommy Lucchese who had recruited him, perhaps due to the pair working together previously as part of the 107th Street Gang. During this early stage of his career with the Lucchese crime family, Corallo worked closely with mobster Johnny Dio, who ran labor racketeering operations for the family. At 28 years old, Corallo served his first sentence in prison, having been caught by police in possession of a narcotics cache worth around $150,000. Slammed with a narcotics charge, Corallo served a six-month term on Rikers Island in 1941.

Two years after his first prison sentence, Corallo had "[risen] in the ranks of the Lucchese family," having been promoted to *capo*, which came with his own crew of soldiers (Feuer, 2000). Corallo moved his operations and his crew from his old neighborhood of East Harlem to Queens, where he set about proving his worth to Gagliano and Lucchese. Having created a strong bond with Dio since early in his criminal career, and considering that Dio's fingers were already firmly in the pies of numerous labor unions, the two began exerting their power and expanding their influence.

After a while, Corallo and Dio controlled a substantial number of local International Brotherhood of Teamsters chapters, as well as local chapters of the Conduit Workers Union, the United Textile Workers Union, and the Brotherhood of Painters and Decorators. Corallo and Dio's use for these local chapters was twofold: firstly, it allowed them to wrangle lucrative deals with trucking companies; secondly, it gave them immense influence over the rank-and-file members of the chapters, allowing for the pair to exploit the chapter's decisions and outcomes. Suffice to say, Corallo and Dio's labor racketeering made the Lucchese crime family millions of dollars, putting Corallo in extremely good stead with his superiors.

As a slight aside, one may have noticed that Corallo's nickname is quite unique and arguably more imaginative than the standard given in the American Mafia. His nickname stems from his strange ability to avoid convictions. From 1941 to 1960, Corallo was arrested 12 times for a plethora of different crimes, although none of these arrests led to trials or convictions. Lucchese, who had by then succeeded Gagliano as Boss of the Lucchese crime family, was amazed by Corallo's perceived ability. Allegedly, after one of these many dodges, Lucchese stated, "Tony ducks again." After this comment, the name stuck and Corallo was forever known as Anthony "Tony Ducks" Corallo.

In 1957, the United States Senate set up the "U.S. Senate Select Committee on Improper Activities in Labor and Management in order to, amongst other things, investigate the extent of criminal activities in labor-management relations" ("Guide to Senate

Records: Chapter 18 1946-1968," 2016). Being heavily involved in labor racketeering, Corallo was an individual that the committee were adamant to question. They did just that in 1959 when Corallo was called to testify before them.

Specifically, the committee wanted Corallo to explain the theft of $70,000 from a local Teamsters union using the names of deceased mobsters. Corallo made no attempt to explain himself and, throughout the two-hour interrogation, apparently pled the Fifth Amendment (referencing the Self-Incrimination clause) 120 times. In 1961, law enforcement finally managed to pin Corallo down, as he was indicted on charges of bribery.

Corallo had attempted to get a bankruptcy fraud case against one of his associates dropped by bribing both Supreme Court Justice J. Vincent Keogh and former U.S. attorney Elliot Kanaher. This was a conviction that even the infamous "Tony Ducks" could not dodge, and in 1962, Corallo was convicted of bribery and sentenced to two years in prison. When Lucchese died in 1967, Corallo was the favorite to succeed him as Lucchese had indicated him as such personally. However, Corallo could not immediately take leadership as he was in prison for a completely separate bribery conviction. It transpired that Corallo had bribed the then water commissioner of New York City, James L. Marcus, "in exchange for contracts to clean and repair parts of the city's water reservoir system" (Feuer, 2000). Corallo was ultimately sentenced to three years for bribery in 1968, making him ineligible to take over leadership of the Lucchese crime family.

As we have previously seen, Carmine Tramunti was chosen in Corallo's stead and was almost immediately barraged with indictments and convictions, finally being sentenced to a long prison term for his role in the French Connection narcotics trafficking scheme. When Tramunti was sentenced in 1973, Corallo finally took his place officially as the Boss of the Lucchese crime family.

The Family Under Corallo

When Corallo took charge of the Lucchese crime family, he intended to maintain the philosophy of his former mentor Tommy Lucchese, who pulled the Lucchese crime family up to a place of power, wealth, and respect. Corallo had served under Lucchese during this rise and, after appointing Salvatore "Tom Mix" Santoro as his underboss and Christopher "Christie Tick" Furnari as *consigliere*, he began his mission to continue where Lucchese left off. As Boss, Corallo was "widely regarded as an old-time don, a crusty but gentle son of La Cosa Nostra, who believed in honor, staked his reputation on his word… and considered loose lips a treachery worse than murder" (Feuer, 2000). We have seen a prime example of the last on this list from Corallo's demeanor during his questioning by the United States Senate in 1959.

Corallo also "continued the Lucchese family's long-standing penchant for shying away from the limelight," with one former law enforcement investigator stating, "In a time when a mob boss' suit could light up a room, he [Corallo] was given to wearing grey cardigan sweaters" (Feuer, 2000). Personally, those who knew Corallo described him as someone who "cherished his privacy and that his family was the dearest thing to him in the world," adding that he was a quiet man who enjoyed the simple things in life, such as "pasta, opera, and working in the garden outside his home"

(Feuer, 2000). Corallo owned a luxury home in Oyster Bay Cove, Long Island, where he lived with his wife and two children. Taking these descriptions of Corallo in mind, it paints a picture of a man wildly juxtaposed to his profession. However, it was a profession that he took seriously, and Corallo had been and never was afraid to exert his power when necessary.

It is safe to say that the Lucchese crime family prospered under Corallo. Already being heavily involved in the labor rackets during his time as a *capo*, Corallo had garnered a great deal of power over the various labor unions of New York City and had become friendly with powerful figures such as Jimmy Hoffa, who was a labor union leader and president of the Teamsters at the time.

Corallo also expanded the Lucchese crime family's enterprises, being particularly interested in "the private trash-hauling business and in million-dollar Manhattan construction projects" (Feuer, 2000). Using his influence over the labor unions to assist, Corallo created rackets in both the construction and garbage industries. Corallo also called upon his many contacts to assist in his expansion of the Lucchese crime family's enterprises; union official Bernie Adelstein assisted in the creation of the front company Private Sanitation Industry Association for Corallo's expansion into the garbage industry and longtime Lucchese *capo* (and *consigliere* to Carmine Tramunti) Paul Vario and his crew helped Corallo maintain and gain even more power at John F. Kennedy airport (previously known as Idlewild airport). Corallo tasked his underboss Santoro to supervise all rackets related to labor unions and construction. Corallo also held the New Jersey faction of the Lucchese crime family in high regard and made sure he was personally involved in its leadership decisions. He inducted both Anthony "Tumac" Accetturo and Michael "Mad Dog" Taccetta into the Lucchese crime family himself, quickly promoting them to leadership positions within the faction. This sub-organization of the Lucchese crime family went on to control the majority of loan sharking and illegal gambling operations in Newark.

It is quite evident that Corallo led the Lucchese crime family to further prosperity, maintaining established enterprises as well as creating new avenues that proved beneficial and lucrative. Well-liked and respected by criminal and law enforcement alike, it seemed that Corallo's tenure as Boss would be seen in a similar fashion to that of his mentor Tommy Lucchese. But it was not to be, as Corallo had one particular habit that caused an avalanche that destabilized not only the Lucchese crime family but the entire American Mafia.

Bugging the Jaguar

Corallo never discussed Mafia business during sit-downs or in public. He was aware that law enforcement could be listening and monitoring his conversations, so he was careful as to what he said both out in the public sphere or in an environment that could be easily compromised. Of course, being in Corallo's profession required him to talk business, sometimes at length, so he would only talk Mafia business from the car phone of his Jaguar as he was being driven around New York City.

Although sharing the responsibility of chauffeuring Corello with Aniello Migliore, Salvatore "Sal" Avellino was regularly present with Corello in the Jaguar, driving him around and being privy to his business conversations. Avellino was Corello's right-hand man, helping to maintain a stranglehold on the garbage and waste disposal industries for the Lucchese crime family.

Despite his loyalty to Corello, it was Avellino that law enforcement used to incriminate the Lucchese Boss. The New York State Organized Crime Task Force (OCTF) was attempting to gather evidence against Avellino. Knowing that he assisted Corello in maintaining the Lucchese crime family's waste disposal racket in Long Island, the OCTF acquired the help of garbage-hauling business owner Robert Kubecka.

Kubecka had resisted the mob's control over the industry throughout the 1970s and was the target of extensive extortion attempts and intimidation tactics for his refusal to cooperate. When approached by the OCTF in 1982 and asked to wear a wire when next he met with the mobsters, Kubecka readily agreed. The material Kubecka gathered from this was enough for a judge to grant the OCTF permission to place a wiretap on Avellino's home phone. The conversations law enforcement heard from this wiretap were neither useful nor incriminating. They did, however, garner at least one sliver of useful information: that Avellino was Corello's personal chauffeur.

In 1983, members of the OCTF managed to plant "a listening device inside the dashboard of Avellino's black Jaguar as it sat in a parking lot of the Huntington Town House, a Long Island catering hall" whilst Avellino and his wife were attending a dinner and dance evening (Feuer, 2000). Then, law enforcement needed to only wait until the next time Avellino picked up Corallo. This bug in the Jaguar proved to be a proverbial goldmine for the OCTF, as they listened in and recorded conversations between Corallo and both Avellino and other mobsters. Topics included the Lucchese crime family rackets and enterprises, such as labor racketeering, murder, and drug trafficking, as well as all law enforcement needed to know about the shadowy Mafia Commission and its internal structure, hierarchy, history, and relations to the wider American Mafia.

One conversation recorded was of Avellino telling Corallo that "they were being followed by a car, probably because the authorities believed that Corallo controlled the toxic waste disposal industry. Corallo gave a simple response: 'They're right," he said' (Feuer, 2000). This gave law enforcement a mine of invaluable evidence to bring against not just Corallo but the entire leadership of the American Mafia. The tapes collected through the listening device in Corallo's Jaguar "became one of the primary building blocks of the federal case against Corallo," along with almost the entire leadership of the Five Families of New York (Feuer, 2000). The trial that would come out of these taped conversations would be the first of its kind, with "no previous trial [having] ever focused directly on the highest levels of Mafia leadership, and some investigators have said that the five families never truly recovered" (Feuer, 2000).

The Mafia Commission Trial

In February of 1985, Corallo and "two other Five Families Bosses, Anthony "Fat Tony" Salerno (of the Genovese crime family) and Carmine "Junior" Persico (of the Colombo crime family), were indicted in what would become known as the Mafia Commission Trial" (Lubasch, 1985). Corallo was actually in hospital at the time of his indictment and not arrested until he was released days later. The three family bosses were not the only ones indicted, however, with the final list being Corallo, Salerno, Persico, Salvatore Santaro (Corallo's underboss), Christopher Furnari (Corallo's *consigliere*), Gennaro Langella (Persico's underboss), Ralph Scopo (Colombo family soldier), and Anthony Indelicato (Bonanno family soldier). There were originally three more defendants in the indictment but they had gone on to die by natural causes or otherwise. The three mobsters were "Paul Castellano, Gambino family boss (murdered December 16th, 1985); Aniello Dellacroce, Gambino family underboss (died of cancer December 2nd, 1985); and Stephano Cannone, Bonanno family *consigliere* (died of natural causes September 1985)" (Knight, 2021). By the time the trial came around in 1986, the indictments against the mobsters had expanded to 25, including charges such as extortion, narcotics, and murder. Right before the trial was set to begin, the defendants were called to a bond hearing where "magistrate Michael Dollinger read out an obligatory statement warning that if the defendants should threaten any witness in the case, their bail would be forfeited. Christie 'Tick' Furnari asked, 'What witnesses?' His attorney quickly led him out" (Knight, 2021). Furnari's comment here is a great indicator of how the Mafia Commission Trial proceeded, a circus that the media and public loved to watch, and they were never left disappointed.

On September 8th, 1986, the Mafia Commission Trial began. Persico (who had decided to represent himself in the trial) suggested some directives to presiding Judge Richard Owen, including attempting to tell Owen how to question prospective jurors. Owen shut this down, replying to Persico, "I'm accustomed to asking people questions in language that they can understand and answer" (Knight, 2021).

During the trial, the prosecution was "intent on showing that the Commission was a criminal enterprise and that each of the defendants was a member of the Commission, or of an entity directly under its control" (Knight, 2021). U.S. attorney Michael Chertoff told the jury on the trial that, "It's not romantic, not like TV, the movies, or books… You'll see them fighting, back-stabbing each other. The Commission was dominated by a single principle: greed" (Knight, 2021). The defense attorneys tasked with proving the innocence of the mobsters had to think outside of the box. They were wholly aware that the prosecution would "emphasize how the defendants were all going to deny the Mafia's existence," so defense attorney Samuel Dawson told the jury, "This case is not about whether an organization is in existence, known as the Mafia or La Cosa Nostra. There is, right here in New York City" (Knight, 2021). Dawson stressed the point that there was no evidence to suggest the defendants were guilty and that just because the defendants were members of the Mafia did not mean that they had committed the crimes charged in this particular case. Persico also got up and spoke to the jury as he was representing himself. Wearing "gold-rimmed glasses and a black pin-striped suit," his plan was to "win the jury over with charm, self-abasement, and empathy," although he used most of his time speaking to the jury aiming criticism at the prosecution and the government (Knight, 2021).

On the first full day of the trial, the jurors were informed that they would hear taped conversations of the defendants and their associates. The first tape to be played would be those recorded in Avellino's Jaguar between him and Corallo. The jury listened to these recordings through headphones and following transcripts as "some of the recorded conversations were, at times, difficult to understand" (Knight, 2021). Wanting to plant a seed of doubt in the jurors' heads, the defense "immediately disputed the audibility of some of the tapes, and questioned the accuracy of the transcripts," knowing that they only had to get one juror to side with them to win the case (Knight, 2021).

In the tape recording, Corallo and Avellino can be heard discussing problems with members of the Lucchese crime family dealing in narcotics, which was not approved by the Commission. When Avellino asks, "How should the dealers be handled?" Corallo replies, "We should kill them" (Knight, 2021). This evidence was damning, but it was not the only recording of Corallo to be played. In another recorded conversation, "Salerno complained to… Corallo about a lack of appreciation and respect among the rank-and-file mobsters" (Knight, 2021). When Salerno goes on to tell Corallo about a specific underling who disrespected him, Corallo offers a solution, "Shoot him. Get rid of them, shoot them, kill them. It's disgusting" (Knight, 2021). Near the end of the proceedings, Persico gave his closing statement. He "compared the trial to a bus tour through Tinseltown," asserting that they "had no direct evidence" against any of the defendants, with Dawson adding that "the prosecution had presented guesses, speculations, and assumptions but no solid evidence" (Knight, 2021). The closing arguments occurred on Friday, 14th November 1986, and the jury went into deliberation over the weekend. The next Wednesday, and after 10 weeks of trial, the jury "delivered a crippling blow to the defendants, finding all eight guilty of racketeering, conspiracy, and operating a Commission that ruled the Mafia throughout the United States" (Knight, 2021). When the sentences came, they were just as devastating. All but one defendant was sentenced to 100 years in prison, including Corallo, Santoro, and Furnari.

As the trial dragged on, Corallo realized that the Lucchese crime family hierarchy was in danger as it became more and more obvious that Santoro, Furnari, and himself were going to be convicted and sentenced. It was not just the prison sentences that concerned Corallo; it was also the fact that all three of the Lucchese crime family's top men were at an advanced age and the sentences they were facing would essentially guarantee that they die in prison.

An emergency meeting was called at Furnari's home, where the Lucchece hierarchy discussed who would take their place as the leadership of the family. Corallo had originally chosen *capo* Anthony Luongo to take his place, but Luongo disappeared under mysterious circumstances soon after. With this, the choice came down to Vittorio "Vic" Amuso or Anthony "Gaspipe" Casso, both members of Funari's old crew during his time as a *capo*. Amuso eventually won out, and it was decided that he would take control of the Lucchese crime family when Corallo was sent to prison. Corallo's fears were realized in 1987 when he was sentenced as part of the Mafia Commission Trial. It was a cruel twist of irony that Corallo, a man known for his ability to duck criminal charges, was ultimately brought low by a charge that he himself was a prominent architect in. Corallo did indeed die in prison in the year 2000, with natural causes felling him at the Federal Medical Center in Missouri.

CHAPTER 6

A RUTHLESS STRANGLEHOLD: VITTORIO AMUSO AND ANTHONY CASSO

From its inception through to the late 1980s, the Lucchese crime family held the title of one of the most stable and peaceful crime organizations operating in the United States, considering its status as a Mafia crime family and member of the powerful Five Families of New York. From Gaetano Reina through to Anthony Corallo, the Lucchese leadership put stock in the philosophy of subtlety, keeping violence low, wallets full, and law enforcement attention to an absolute minimum. Corallo's indictment as part of the Mafia Commission Trial changed this standard drastically, however, opening up the floodgates for one of the most violent and bloody regimes in American Mafia history. This unhinged and tumultuous era was headed by a pair of ruthless mobsters: Boss Vittorio Amuso and his underboss Anthony Casso. In this chapter, we will explore the beginnings of both Amuso and Casso, their rise and eventual stranglehold over the Lucchese crime family, the two New York City police detectives who moonlighted as contract killers and directly answered to the pair, and how even prison could not stop them from exerting their terrifying control over organized crime.

Amuso and Casso

Vittorio "Little Vic" Amuso hailed from Brooklyn, where he was born in 1934 and spent his formative years. In the late 1940s, Amuso was first introduced to Lucchese crime family *capo* Anthony Corallo, who would later choose Amuso to succeed him as Boss. In his early work for the Lucchese crime family, Amuso took the role of chauffeur and bodyguard to Carmine Tramunti. In regard to his personal life, Amuso lived with his wife Barbara and child (a daughter) in Queens, New York City. Amuso would not stick around with the Lucchese crime family, becoming an enforcer for the Colombo crime family (then called the Profaci crime family) mobster Joseph "Crazy Joe" Gallo.

Amuso was caught in the middle of a power struggle when Gallo and his brother (who were being supported by the Mafia Commission alliance of Tommy Lucchese and Carlo Gambino at the time) rebelled against Profaci Boss Giuseppe Profaci in both a grab for power and due to a disagreement concerning profit cuts from criminal activities ran by the Gallo brothers. Amuso, of course, sided with Gallo, allegedly murdering multiple members of Profaci's crew, but was sent to prison, along with Gallo and several others, in the early 1960s on extortion charges.

When Gallo was released from prison in 1971, he continued his crusade against the Profaci family, which by then had adopted the name of the Colombo crime family. This vengeful war ended in the shooting of Colombo Boss Joseph Colombo in 1971 and then Gallo's own murder a year later. Out celebrating his birthday in Little Italy, Gallo was mercilessly shot to death. When Gallo was assassinated, many of his associates peeled off to join other crime families. In 1972, Amuso did just this, joining the Lucchese crime family as an associate linked with the 19th Hole Crew; the *capo* of the crew was none other than Christopher "Christie Tick" Funari, who would later serve as *consigliere* to Anthony Corallo and assist in Amuso's rise to the top.

Born in May of 1942 in South Brooklyn, Anthony "Gaspipe" Casso was the youngest of three children. Casso spent the majority of his youth "shooting birds off tenement buildings... with a .22 caliber rifle that he'd rigged with a silencer" (Margaritoff, 2021). He became quite the sharpshooter, even making money by killing predatory birds for local pigeon keepers. His links to organized crime were apparent early on, as Casso's godfather Salvatore Callinbrano had been a captain in the Genovese crime family and his father, Michael, had a record of burglaries in the 1940s.

In all fairness to Casso's father, he had left his criminal life behind and worked legitimately as a longshoreman. Casso joined him in this occupation, dropping out of school at 16 to work alongside his father. Whilst Michael consistently urged Casso to stay clear of criminal life, Casso admired both his father's and godfather's criminal past, even taking on the nickname "Gaspipe" after the rumored favorite weapon of his father's. Criminality was clearly a profession that Casso admired, so much so that he regularly got into "teenage scraps with his fledgling South Brooklyn Boys gang" (Margaritoff, 2021). With the gang, he was arrested in 1958 when he was involved in a scuffle with an Irish-American gang. Attempting to drag his son onto a better path, Michael visited his son in prison and had a conversation with him. His pleas fell on deaf ears, however, as Casso had caught the attention of Furnari and, at the age of 21, he was inducted into the Lucchese crime family, joining Furnari in his 19th Hole Crew. It was here that Casso met fellow rising Lucchese mobster Vittorio Amuso.

As a partnership, Amuso and Casso quickly rose up the ranks of the Lucchese crime family, as well as racked up a number of arrests and convictions. Both mobsters became full members of the Lucchese crime family during the 1970s.

Casso started his Mafia career in loan sharking, gambling, and drug dealing. Whilst working on a bookmaking operation for Furnari at Brooklyn Docks, Casso revealed his dark sense of humor. A dockworker mentioned to Casso about his recently bought shoes. In response, Casso "took over a forklift and dropped about 500 pounds of cargo on the [dockworker's] feet and broke most of his toes", claiming that "he wanted to see how good the new boots were" (Margaritoff, 2021). From 1965 to 1977, Casso was arrested five times on a multitude of charges "ranging from assault with a gun to heroin trafficking" (Margaritoff, 2021). In 1972, Amuso was arrested in possession of a switchblade and a file full of parole documents by law enforcement officers. He was charged with selling prison inmates paroles from upwards of $20,000.

Whilst infamous enough individually, the pair hit their criminal stride when they worked together. As a team under the Lucchese banner, they "extorted construction contractors and trucking companies for labor union peace, trafficked drugs, and ran gambling rackets" (Margaritoff, 2021). Along with other members of the 19th Hole Crew, "they formed a burglary ring comprised of safe-crackers called The Bypass Gang," with authorities indicating that the gang stole around $100 million by the end of the 1980s.

In 1977, the pair were arrested in connection to a drug smuggling operation out of Bangkok, Thailand. Amuso was caught by authorities with three pounds of heroin on his person, and it was alleged that the operation was run by Amuso, Casso, and two other Lucchese crime family associates. When Furnari was promoted to *consigliere* under Corallo, he asked Casso to take over as *capo* of the 19th Hole Crew. However, Casso preferred the idea of becoming Furnari's aide-de-camp (essentially a personal assistant and direct aide). Casso also convinced Furnari to make Amuso the *capo* of the crew instead. Furnari agreed to this, raising both Amuso and Casso's reputations in the Lucchese family further. As successful as the pair's criminal endeavors and rise through the ranks had been up until this point, the mid-1980s would see a chain of events that would rocket both Amuso and Casso into the annals of American Mafia history.

The Duo With Iron Fists

In December of 1985, the *capo* of the Gambino crime family Frank DeCicco approached Casso with a plan; he wanted assistance in a coup within the Gambino crime family. *Capo* John Gotti, who had worked with Casso on multiple criminal operations, was leading a charge to assassinate current Gambino Boss Paul Castellano. This coup came at a time of great disturbance in the foundations of the American Mafia, mainly due to the ongoing Mafia Commission Trial, and the conspirators were searching for support from individuals who were part of the other member organizations of the Five Families of New York.

DeCicco allegedly returned from his discussion with Casso with the idea that Casso would give his full support to the coup. Casso, however, had a different version of the discussion's outcome. Casso, wary that the conspirators had failed to ask for the Mafia Commission's approval to assassinate Castellano, who "regulated such acts among New York's Five Families," attempted to convince DiCicco to approach the Mafia Commission to ask permission before going through with the overthrowing of Castellano (Margaritoff, 2021). If they went ahead without permission, Casso warned that they would be murdered in retaliation for breaking the Mafia code. Whether this difference in what was discussed was due to crossed wires or simply Casso trying to cover his own back after the fact is unknown.

What is clear, however, is that Castellano's murder went ahead without permission. Both "Lucchese boss Anthony Corallo and Genovese boss Vincent Gigante were furious and hired Anthony Casso to seek retribution" (Margaritoff, 2021). Bringing Amuso along with him to handle the assassinations, the pair decided to use a car bomb to deal with both Gotti and DiCicco. Using information acquired from Gambino *capo* Daniel Marino, "Casso and Amuso learned of a meeting that Gotti had set at the Veterans and Friends club in Brooklyn on April 13, 1986" (Margaritoff, 2021). Knowing that DiCicco (who was now Gotti's underboss) would be driving Gotti to the engagement, the pair "had an unaffiliated gang rig the Buick Electra… with explosives" (Margaritoff, 2021). Reportedly, Casso and Amuso watched the rigged car from their own vehicle parked close by. However, Gotti canceled his appearance last minute, and the bomb only killed DeCicco.

When the Mafia Commission Trial indicted the highest ranking members of the Lucchese family, namely Boss Anthony Corallo, underboss Salvatore Santoro, and *consigliere* Christopher Furnari, the leadership scrambled to find those to succeed them as the outcome of the trial was looking to be dire. As a first choice, Corallo chose *capo* Anthony "Buddy" Luongo to replace him, with Luongo having been the protege of underboss Santoro. Seeing Luongo as their only barrier to power over the Lucchese crime family, Amuso and Casso lured him to a meeting at a bar in Brooklyn before convincing him to go with Amuso to an apartment close by. When there, Amuso and Cassa assassinated Luongo by shooting him in the head. To Corallo, Santoro, and Furnari, it was as if Luongo had vanished off the face of the earth.

By late 1986, with their sentences looming, Corallo and the leadership of the Lucchese crime family held a meeting at Furnari's home in order to confirm their replacements. Corallo preferred Casso to succeed him. However, just like he had done with the 19th Hole Gang, Casso refused the promotion and convinced the leadership that Amuso should be the new Boss. After the Mafia Commission Trial sentenced Corallo, Santoro, and Furnari to 100-year prison terms, Amuso officially succeeded Corallo as Boss of the Lucchese crime family, with Casso filling many roles throughout the late 1980s and early 1990s, including both *consigliere* and underboss.

Amuso and Casso instituted a brutal and violent reign over the Lucchese crime family from Amuso's appointment as Boss in 1987 through to the early 1990s and beyond. After assisting in the assassination attempt on John Gotti, the pair held an intense rivalry with the Gambino crime family and a strong alliance with fellow conspirator and Genovese crime family Boss Vincent Gigante. Both heavily involved in labor racketeering, drug trafficking, murder, and extortion, the two men aggressively expanded the Lucchese crime family's criminal enterprise and unceremoniously slaughtered anyone who dared stand in their way, perceived or otherwise.

One of their most infamous actions, and one that acts as a microcosm for their reign, came at the very beginning. In the late 1980s, the Jersey Crew (the firm favorite family branch of Anthony Corallo) had become extremely powerful, controlling profitable rackets across New Jersey. Amuso and Casso began demanding a larger share in the crew's rackets, as the pair were not happy with the current annual $50,000 payment coming from the Jersey Crew. After Amuso and Casso asked for a 50% cut, the Jersey Crew leader Anthony 'Tumac" Accetturo refused the demand. Amuso was furious at this denial, immediately stripping Accetturo of his rank as leader of the crew. In 1988, Amuso called for all members of the Jersey Crew to meet in Brooklyn. Whilst some members did indeed show up, they were paranoid that Amuso and Casso would murder them all, so they soon fled. This mass exodus only served to further anger Amuso, who was so irate that he ordered the whole Jersey Crew to be killed. This order went down in Mafia history as the "whack Jersey" order. What came next was nothing short of a massacre, with Amuso and Casso murdering anyone who they even slightly suspected as a rival or turncoat.

Many members of the Jersey Crew did eventually return to the Lucchese crime family, and Amuso's hunt for former leader

Accetturo failed, although most definitely not through lack of trying. He had sent hitmen as far as Florida seeking Accetturo, but he had been arrested and was being held in New Jersey. Amuso and Casso also raked in masses of profit from numerous different enterprises, making both the Lucchese crime family and themselves extremely wealthy.

These enterprises were vast in scope, from illegal video game machines and extortion of local companies to owning rackets in the construction supply and garment businesses and receiving kickbacks from air freight carriers. To put the sheer amount of wealth the pair were amassing into perspective, some instances must be described: $800,000 from the Colombo family due to assistance in the robbery of steel from a construction site, $600,000 from the Gambino crime family due to allowing them access to a Lucchese family-owned housing contractor, and control of the Velentzas Organization which netted them another $683,000 in protection money. This list, as one can most likely imagine, is far from extensive, with the pair filling the Lucchese crime family's coffers almost as fast as they could spend it. The word "almost" here is used specifically, as Casso was known to enjoy the finer things in life. He "spent $30,000 on suits and racked up $1,000 restaurant bills" (Margaritoff, 2021). He also began construction on "a $1 million mansion in the Mill Basin area of Brooklyn" (Margaritoff, 2021). The duo were on top of the world as the 1980s became the 1990s, but their bloody and destructive spree had not gone unnoticed.

The Mafia Cops

Before we continue on in the saga of a Lucchese crime family run by the iron fists of Amuso and Casso, it seems a prevalent time in this exploration to switch the perspective in order to fully comprehend the stranglehold that the two mobsters had over the criminal underworld of New York City. Whilst there are indeed many stories that involve the corruption of law enforcement, this particular one is potent as it encompasses the very real danger of criminal influence on societal institutions, especially when that institution is supposed to hold up and enforce the law. The story of police detectives Stephen Caracappa and Louis Eppolito represents the ability of organized crime to permeate all levels of society, its shadowy influence seeping through even the smallest of cracks.

Louis Eppolito was born in Brooklyn in 1948, the son of registered nurse Theresa and Gambino crime family associate Ralph. The "rotund Eppolito" had links to organized crime that went further than his father, with his uncle and cousin being members of the Gambino crime family also (Celona, 2020). During his formative years, and due to his familial connections, he came into contact with many mobsters. He applied to the New York City Police Department in 1969 at 21 years of age. On his application, he lied by stating that he had no family members who were involved in organized crime. The "tall, thin Caracappa" had been working for the New York City Police Department since the late 1970s in the Organized Crime Homicide Unit (Celona, 2020). It was around this time that Eppolito also rose to the rank of detective. By 1985, the police detectives had joined Anthony Casso's payroll. They were paid "$4,000 per month [to tip] Casso off about snitches and coming incidents" (Margaritoff, 2021). This was not the extent of their involvement, however, as they essentially "moonlighted as Mafia hitmen" (Celona, 2020). In 1986, the detectives kidnapped and delivered James Hydell (a Gambino crime family associate) directly to Casso to be murdered. This was in retaliation for an attempt on Casso's life, and the pair would "eventually murder a total of eight people for Casso" (Margaritoff, 2021). One of these murders was of Lucchese crime family associate Bruno Facciolo, who was suspected of being an informant. After murdering Facciolo, "the two shoved a canary into the mouth of the corpse" for federal agents to find at the crime scene (Celona, 2020). Eppolito and Caracappa also murdered the Gambino crime family *capo* Edward Lino on the orders of Casso, pulling Lino over in his car and shooting him through the window.

In the mid-1990s, after a series of law enforcement moves against the crime families of New York, Eppolito and Caracappa "[retired] as lifelong friends to the same cell block in Las Vegas" (Celona, 2020). Caracappa went on to work as a corrections officer in Las Vegas, whilst Eppolito found a short career in acting. Eppolito had a chance meeting with actor Joe Pesci at a restaurant frequented by celebrities, which led to Eppolito appearing in movies *Goodfellas*, *Predator 2*, and *Lost Highway*. Ironically, after retiring from the police force in 1990, Eppolito authored a book titled *Mafia Cop: The Story of an Honest Cop Whose Family Was the Mob*. In the book, he claimed that he struggled with the pull of the Mafia whilst working as a New York City Police Department detective. Whilst in Las Vegas with Caracappa, Eppolito found a job selling automobiles, where he entertained his colleagues with crime scene photos from his policing days. Whilst the crooked detectives may have felt secure at their retirement hideaway in Las Vegas, federal authorities had been on to them as early as 1985, when Casso first hired them.

After a long investigation, both Eppolito and Caracappa were arrested in 2005, charged with racketeering, obstruction of justice, and extortion, as well as eight counts of murder and conspiracy. A key witness in their conviction was one Burton Kaplan, who had acted as the go-between in communications between the detectives and Casso. In 2009, they were sentenced; Eppolito received a life sentence plus 100 years and Caracappa a life sentence plus 80 years, and "both died, unrepentant, in federal prison" (Celona, 2020). Throughout the late 1980s and early 1990s, Eppolito and Caracappa allowed Amuso and Casso to stay one step ahead of law enforcement, as well as root out any potential informants within their own ranks, uncaring as to whether they truly were snitches or not. The crooked detectives "disgraced their badges like no one else in NYPD history," showing that even those who are supposed to serve and protect may only do so for themselves.

A Boss and Underboss Captured

When we last left off, Amuso and Casso were flying high, raking in masses of profit and exercising almost total control over the criminal underworld. However, their tactics were less than subtle and, unlike their predecessors, eschewed the Lucchese crime family's philosophy of keeping a low profile. Neither Casso nor Amuso cared "if [they] violated sacred Mafia codes [or] killed civilians on the mere suspicion they were informants," carving a bloody path through New York City and beyond (Margaritoff, 2021). It would be this style of leadership that put the pair of mobsters directly in the limelight of law enforcement.

In May of 1990, "Casso's NYPD sources tipped him off about a racketeering indictment by the Brooklyn Federal Court (Margaritoff, 2021). In the years prior, the Five Families of New York had been involved in rigging bids of window fitting contracts doled out by the New York City Housing Authority. Leading the Lucchese crime family in this venture, Amuso and Casso had been implicated in the subsequent fitting of thousands of windows at inflated prices whilst also receiving kickbacks for each window installed through their stranglehold on the labor unions. The pair were in danger of being surprised by authorities and apprehended. With this heads up, "both Casso and Amuso went on the run" (Margaritoff, 2021). Feeling it necessary to leave the Lucchese crime family with a temporary mouthpiece to look to whilst they waited for the heat from law enforcement to die down, Amuso and Casso appointed an acting Boss to lead in their absence. The man who the mobsters chose would go on to achieve the title of one of the most high-profile government informants in American Mafia history.

CHAPTER 7
THE BOSS OF SNITCHES: ALPHONSE "LITTLE AL" D'ARCO

The Mafia code is stringent. It highlights honor, loyalty, and respect amongst its most valued tenants. There is also "*omerta*, the code of silence" (Oxford University Press, 1989). It demands its followers not to cooperate with the authorities or outsiders, not interfere with the criminal activities of others, and even ignore the very existence of organized crime when questioned on such matters. The Mafia, or at least the romanticized version of it that exists in the public consciousness, takes this code very seriously, with many prospective members swearing to it through a blood oath. Of course, even with these strict parameters, there have been a surprising amount of Mafia members who have broken this oath. In the eyes of the organization they betrayed, they are snitches, squealers, and rats deserving of painful death. If this is the punishment, then one could reasonably ask what it is that drives individuals to turn on their surrogate families and run into the arms of law enforcement. One answer may be that, as honorable and admirable as the Mafia code is on paper, perhaps it is more complicated to abide by the rules in practice. When one is facing the reality of spending the rest of their life in a prison cell, the honor and respect of *omertia* may very well dissipate in favor of legal immunity and reduced sentences.

Regardless of the reasons, of which there could be admittedly many, Mafia members have been turning on their allies for the majority of organized crime history, and not just the rank-and-file soldiers, but also those all the way up in the lofty heights of criminal royalty. When Amuso and Casso went into hiding in 1990, they installed an unassuming Lucchese crime family member who would become the first Boss of an organized crime family to become a rat: Alphonse "Little Al" D'Arco.

In this chapter, we will explore the history of Alphonse D'Arco, his installment as acting Boss of the Lucchese crime family, his dealings with both Amuso and Casso whilst acting as their mouthpiece, and his eventual turn to becoming a government informant.

Alphonse "Little Al" D'Arco

Young Alphonse D'Arco was surrounded by the criminal side of life. Born in Brooklyn, he grew up "a few blocks from the Navy Yard, then a hub of underworld hustles" (Robbins & Capeci, 2019). Whilst he had an uncle in the mob, his father was a legitimate businessman, running a small basement dye shop in the area and working with the garment industry. However, the call of the criminal profession continued to follow D'Arco as, above his father's shop, a local hoodlum had a bookmaking operation and the young D'Arco was awestruck and enamored by the bookmaker's clientele. This call proved too enticing, it seems, as D'Arco committed his first crime at the age of 12, that being the robbing of a furniture factory. This first foray into criminality earned him a beating from his father, but this did not deter the young D'Arco, who began work for a local candy store operator who spent his downtime gambling and peddling stolen goods.

For a time, he did attend a Catholic grammar school but, by the age of 15, he had dropped out. Soon after, he enlisted in the United States Army, seemingly his only attempt to work legitimately. He served in the Korean War, though he did not see combat, spending his two years stationed at an isolated airfield near the Arctic Circle on near-continuous guard duty. By 1953, D'Arco had been honorably discharged and was back in New York City. At this time, he got married to his sweetheart Dolores Pellegrino, who "had swept him off his budding young gangster feet when they'd met at a Brooklyn nightclub in 1953" (Robbins & Cipeci, 2019). D'Arco would stay faithful to Dolores throughout his life, and the two had five children together.

In the 1950s, D'Arco would become a part of the Lucchese crime family, joining as an associate of the Vario crew led by *capo* Paul Vario. Before this introduction to the Lucchese crime family, D'Arco had been tutored by mobster Vincenzo "Jimmy Alto" Altomari, who had taught him to "be low key" and to "not stand out" (Robbins & Cipeci, 2019). D'Arco would take these teachings to heart, forming the basis of his demeanor as Boss later in life. At the end of the decade, D'Arco would have his first encounter with Vittorio Amuso. Little is known about their first meeting, which was most likely in passing. However, it is interesting to ponder on what D'Arco may have thought of Amuso, considering what was to come decades later. D'Arco was convicted on drug charges during the 1960s and subsequently spent several years behind bars. When he finally got out, he joined back in with the Lucchese crime family, which was now under the leadership of Anthony Corallo. D'Arco's criminal activities with the family in this period are vast and varied, making him a jack-of-all-trades when it came to crime. He was involved in loan sharking, bookmaking, the dealing of narcotics, tax evasion, arson, and murder, amongst other crimes.

In somewhat of a unique side job considering his criminal career, D'Arco opened a small Italian restaurant in the 1980s. Called *La Donna Rosa*, "it featured recipes that D'Arco, an amateur cook, had learned from his grandparents" (Robbins & Cipeci, 2019). Regular patrons included "Robert De Niro, who studied the moves of the mobsters who dined there, and John F. Kennedy Jr., who sat alone, quietly enjoying lunch during breaks from his duties as an assistant district attorney at the nearby courthouse" (Robbins & Cipeci, 2019). Of course, the restaurant did have its uses for D'Arco's main career, as it was used frequently as a meeting place for Lucchese crime family members. In fact, D'Arco had to turn away "late mayor… Ed Koch… at the door" as "a room full of gangsters were holding a confab there," with D'Arco using the excuse that "it was a private party" (Robbins & Cipeci, 2019). In 1983, D'Arco's extensive involvement in criminal activities caught up with him. He was convicted of heroin trafficking and sentenced to four years. However, he was paroled, being released in 1986.

When D'Arco got back onto the streets of New York City, the duo Amuso and Casso had taken control of the Lucchese crime family. Paul Vario, whose crew D'Arco had joined as a young criminal, died in prison, serving a life sentence. D'Arco was promoted to *capo* of Vario's old crew by Amuso. In 1990, D'Arco was again given more responsibility by Amuso, tasked with creating and organizing a "Lucchese construction panel." This panel's purpose was to oversee Lucchese-controlled unions and construction companies as well as negotiate and coordinate business ventures with other member organizations of the Five Families. Suffice to say that D'Arco was benefitting from the responsibilities being bestowed on him by Amuso and Casso, becoming rather wealthy from the Vario gang's criminal activities as well as his own personal operations. He was then put in charge of collecting tributes to Amuso and Casso from the various Lucchese crews. Allegedly, on one Christmas, D'Arco scrounged up a festive gift of $100,000 for the ruling duo from all the Lucchese *capos*.

At the beginning of the 1990s, Casso received a warning from his NYPD spies that Amuso and himself were about to be indicted in a large racketeering case. Given the time to react, both men went into hiding. However, they required someone to watch over the family whilst they waited for the law enforcement heat to die down, and D'Arco was waiting in the wings.

Installment as Acting Boss

Just before Amuso and himself disappeared, Casso summoned D'Arco to meet with him at John Paul Jones Park in Brooklyn. When he arrived, Casso handed him a list. On said list were phone booth numbers and secret addresses, and D'Arco was told that he was now in charge of the organization until Amuso and himself returned. So it was that, in 1991, D'Arco became the acting Boss of the Lucchese crime family, also sparking an era for the crime organization that saw a carousel of acting bosses come and go. But first, D'Arco would witness the deterioration of both Amuso and

Casso whilst being caught right in the middle of a chaotic period of destruction and bloodshed.

D'Arco was not what one would stereotypically expect from a crime boss, not physically, at least. "He stood just 5 foot 7, hence the nickname" and "unlike flashier Mafia contemporaries such as Gotti, who sauntered through the Little Italy streets with an entourage, D'Arco lived modestly and conservatively" (Robbins & Cipeci, 2019). An FBI surveillance picture of D'Arco proves this point perfectly. In the photo, D'Arco leans shyly out of the opening of a doorway, hands in pockets. The majority of his body is inside, with only his upper body outside. D'Arco was the diametric opposite to the Amuso-Casso partnership, much closer, in fact, to the older Lucchese bosses such as Gagliano and even Tommy Lucchese himself. As true as this is, D'Arco was still expected to be the mouthpiece for Amuso and Casso, whilst also keeping the Lucchese crime family from falling apart. D'Arco could not have prophesied how mutually exclusive these two goals ended up being.

Now at the head of the organization, D'Arco would frequently receive orders from the in-hiding duo of Amuso and Casso, and these orders very quickly began to dissolve into paranoid assassination orders. Having worked so closely with the duo, "D'Arco had first-hand knowledge of how suddenly and viciously Amuso… and Casso… could turn on their longtime partners in crime" (Robbins & Cipeci, 2019). Indeed, just before the duo had been forced into hiding, D'Arco had been ordered to facilitate the murder of Lucchese mobster Bruno Facciola. Amuso and Casso had suspected Facciola of being an informant, and "there was nothing Anthony Casso hated more than informants" (Margaritoff, 2021).

When he found out he was about to be whacked, Facciolo attempted to flee but was subdued and dragged into a garage, where he was both shot and stabbed to death. Amuso and Casso ordered the hitmen to place a canary in the dead man's mouth in order to send a message: if you sing, you die. D'Arco, using the list of addresses given to him by Casso, would meet with him and Amuso whilst they were in hiding, several times at safe houses in Brooklyn and twice in Scranton, Pennsylvania.

Facilitating Murder

D'Arco's facilitation of Facciolo's murder would be the first of many under the orders of Amuso and Casso. In a "spasm of violence, the Lucchese gunman killed a total of 17 men, their bodies left sprawling in underground garages, dumped into landfills, jammed into car trunks or secretly cremated", all of which D'Arco was expected to oversee (Robbins & Cipeci, 2019). Amuso and Casso even gave D'Arco a list of 49 names, all of which were individuals that they wanted to be assassinated. When D'Arco looked over the list, he saw that half of the names were of Lucchese crime family mobsters.

In 1991, D'Arco was ordered to kill Lucchese *capo* Peter "Fat Pete" Chiodo, whom Amuso and Casso had falsely convinced him was a government informant. D'Arco was shocked at the order since he was aware that Chiodo had been a close confidant to Casso. In May of 1991, Chiodo was ambushed as he was working on a car at a gas station in Staten Island. The hitmen, two Lucchese mobsters, shot Chiodo 12 times. Miraculously, despite receiving wounds to his legs, arms, and torso, he survived, with doctors suggesting that it was Chiodo's obesity that saved his vital organs from being ruptured by the bullets. However, Casso and Amuso were not done with Chiodo. They threatened the murder of Chiodo's wife if he testified against them. This threat did not go down well with the majority of the Lucchese crime family members, as it went against American Mafia rules that the families of mobsters were off-limits and should not be involved in any kind of business. Ironically, it was Amuso and Casso's orders and threats that forced Chiodo to testify, as prior to this, he had vehemently resisted any offers of this nature. Chiodo claimed that the threat on his wife's life was the breaking point, and he testified knowing that Amuso and Casso had broken the Mafia oath before he did. Further attacks on Chiodo's extended family cemented the rapidly growing idea amongst Lucchese crime family members that Amuso and Casso were blinded by paranoia and greed and were not acting in a rational way. Chiodo's sister Patricia was shot whilst driving, sustaining injuries to her neck, arm, and back but ultimately surviving. Casso and Amuso also ordered for Lucchese Bronx *capo* Steven Crea to be murdered.

D'Arco came to realize that Amuso and Casso's orders "had little to do with Mafia disloyalty," with "most of the murders [being] an effort to eliminate potential rivals and seize their often lucrative crime operations" (Robbins & Cipeci, 2019). D'Arco was also outraged that Amuso and Casso were breaking traditional Mob rules by "targeting family members of mobsters" (Robbins & Cipeci, 2019).

Many Lucchese crime family members were turning informant as a direct reaction to the unhinged orders of Amuso and Casso. Even D'Arco began to consider this path, becoming more and more convinced that "his number was up as well" (Robbins & Cipeci, 2019). D'Arco was convinced that Amuso and Casso blamed him for the failed hit on Chiodo, who actually had now turned informant for law enforcement. In a meeting in 1991, D'Arco's role as acting Boss was pseudo-dissolved into a four-man *capo* panel. Although D'Arco was on this panel, it was clear to him that Amuso and Casso no longer trusted him and most likely wanted him dead.

D'Arco's suspicions were confirmed when he attended "a business meeting of Lucchese captains in a posh Midtown hotel" (Robbins & Cipeci, 2019). In the middle of the meeting, Lucchese soldier Mike DeSantis appeared, having no real reason for being there. D'Arco spotted DeSantis "stashing a pistol in the bathroom" (Robbins & Cipeci, 2019). D'Arco knew that this was a classic setup for a hit, and that the next person to enter the bathroom would come out shooting. "Believing he was set up to be killed, D'Arco blurted goodbyes and bolted from the hotel room" (Robbins & Cipeci, 2019). When he got outside, he could not find his driver, confirming to him that he was marked by Amuso and Casso for death. The next day, D'Arco and his family fled, and "from a hiding place on Long Island, D'Arco reached out to the FBI" (Robbins & Cipeci, 2019).

Boss-Turned-Informant

When under FBI protection, D'Arco became the first Boss of a crime family, acting or otherwise, to become a government informant, and what he had to say would provide law enforcement with much more than they bargained for. Still, D'Arco was fearful that Casso and Amuso could get to him, knowing that they had at least one corrupt FBI agent on their payroll. D'Arco was still worried that this corrupt agent would turn him over to Casso and Amuso. When federal prosecutors finally went to speak with D'Arco, they found him hiding in the bathroom of his hotel suite. However, when agents got him talking, "out poured a vast stream of Mob knowledge," with D'Arco detailing "the loan shark agreements, the union locals and the mobsters that controlled them, the monthly payoffs from construction companies, the hierarchies of each crime family, even a list of more than two dozen factions in the Sicilian Mafia'" (Robbins & Cipeci, 2019). D'Arco would then go on to testify at numerous trials over the next decade, and his testimonies helped law enforcement land convictions on a swathe of high-ranking organized crime members, including Vincent Gigante and Amuso himself. One FBI agent described D'Arco as "the best," being "the most significant member to cooperate. He really built that bridge for others to cross'" (Robbins & Cipeci, 2019). Along with D'Arco and the other Lucchese crime family members who turned informant, the Lucchese crime family was left all but decimated.

Indeed, "by the time D'Arco and the other cooperators were done testifying, the powerful economic and criminal presence in the city known as the Five Families had been reduced to small groups of aging wiseguys assisted by young wannabes who displayed little talent for organized crime" (Robbins & Cipeci, 2019). Describing his situation after his testimony, D'Arco stated, "I'm still a mobster. But I'm an outlaw, that's all. It's not like they throw you out of the mob when you flip. You're just considered an outlaw. That's what I am" (Robbins & Cipeci, 2019). After his testimony, D'Arco was an excellent witness and never went back to any criminal activities, according to government sources. In March 2019, at 86 years old, D'Arco died of complications related to kidney disease.

D'Arco, Chiodo, and the numerous other Lucchese crime family members who turned informant allowed law enforcement to crack the American Mafia wide open. But one may be wondering what became of Amuso and Casso, who, by all accounts, were still in control of the Lucchese crime family. After going into hiding to avoid the racketeering indictment, the pair began to grow paranoid of those within their own organization. As they both began to spiral downward, it was only a matter of time before they turned on each other. In July of 1991, the FBI captured Amuso in Scranton, Pennsylvania, due to a tipoff from an unknown Lucchese crime family insider. The debate on whether this insider was Casso or not is still argued to this day. Casso was made *de facto* Boss after Amuso's capture, but there are sources that state Casso was determined to find the individual who ratted out Amuso, and he allegedly even sent $250,000 that was due to Amuso to his wife.

What is clear is that Casso, while hungry for power, never wanted to be Boss, consistently refusing top (and arguably exposing positions) in favor of exercising his control from the shadows. On the other hand, Casso was clearly adamant about keeping power and enjoyed the lifestyle of a Mafia high-roller. With Amuso in custody, law enforcement attempted to get him to cooperate. Perhaps having become slightly self-assured due to the number of informants they had already secured, the agents found Amuso impossible to crack. He flatly refused all deals and offers to talk. At his trial in 1992, Amuso's case was decimated by the testimonies of Lucchese crime family informants like D'Arco and Chiodo, and he was charged with all 54 charges brought against him. For this, Amuso received life in prison.

In the end, it did not matter to Amuso as to the murkiness surrounding Casso's involvement in his arrest by the FBI, as Amuso believed that Casso most definitely did tip off law enforcement about his location. In retaliation, Amuso removed Casso as his underboss and declared him an outcast, effectively cutting his longtime partner off from the Lucchese crime family. Casso had managed to stay out of the hands of authorities for two more years than Amuso. However, in 1993, after using a newly-tested technology to trace the location of cell phones, the FBI arrested Casso "as he was coming out of the shower at the home of his mistress in Budd Lake, New Jersey" (Margaritoff, 2021). When they searched the house, FBI agents found a myriad of incriminating evidence, including a rifle, $340,000 in cash, paperwork that detailed the inner workings of the Lucchese crime family, and a list of tribute money received from the various Lucchese crime family crews.

Unlike his former partner, Casso relented to law enforcement pressure and began to talk. He pleaded guilty to a vast amount of criminal charges and ratted out individuals like the Mafia Cops Stephen Caracappa and Louis Eppolito, looking to get a plea deal out of it. He was granted a place in witness protection but "was ejected after a series of bribes and assaults terminated his agreement" (Margaritoff, 2021). Casso was not sentenced until 1998, when he was convicted of a large number of criminal activities, with the judge sentencing him to 455 years in prison without the possibility of parole.

With both its leadership incarcerated and a vast chunk of its membership either working for law enforcement or dead, the Lucchese crime family was in dire straits by the mid-1990s. However, imprisoned Boss Amuso was adamant about keeping control of his organization and he would do so through the mouthpieces that were a series of acting Bosses.

CHAPTER 8

SHIFTING LEADERSHIP: THE ERA OF ACTING BOSSES

It is not unheard of for an acting Boss to take over the operations of a crime family, usually necessary when the official Boss is unable to properly oversee the day-to-day running of the crime family. Of course, this almost exclusively occurs when the Boss has been incarcerated, with the risk of being collared by law enforcement coming with the territory of operating criminal enterprises. Throughout the American Mafia's history, acting Bosses have been appointed sporadically, their reigns lasting for only a short time until the true Boss is free to take their position of leadership once again. The Lucchese crime family, from the mid-1990s, entered into an era that consisted solely of acting Bosses, with each individual being held at the limited mercy of Boss Vittorio Amuso, who was trapped behind bars. His imprisonment, however, did little to hinder him in exerting his control over the Lucchese crime family. In this chapter, we will explore the histories of acting Bosses Joseph DeFede, Steven Crea, and Lou Daidone, as well as the subsequent overhaul in leadership that was unique to the Lucchese crime family.

Joseph "Little Joe" DeFede

Joseph "Little Joe" DeFede was born in 1934 and grew up in Queens, New York City. In his early criminal career, DeFede operated numbers rackets using a hot dog stand as his front business. DeFede was a close friend of Amuso, and the two played handball together often. After Amuso became the Boss of the Lucchese crime family in 1986, DeFede was inducted into the organization. DeFede's "rise and fall in the New York mob can be attributed to Amuso" (People Pill, 2023).

After Amuso was caught and convicted on racketeering charges, he was sentenced to life in prison. Whilst he had been on the run from authorities, Amuso had begun to doubt the loyalty of then-acting Boss Alphonse D'Arco. Convinced that D'Arco would soon turn government informant, Amuso replaced D'Arco with DeFede in 1995, wanting to install a "weaker and more controllable man at the top" ("Joseph DeFede: American mobster," 2023).

Whilst DeFede was indeed the acting Boss of the Lucchese crime family, the panel that had been created to dissipate D'Arco's influence earlier was still in existence, acting as a support structure to DeFede. This panel included Steven Crea, Anthony Baratta, Salvatore Avellino, and Frank Lastorino. Crea was also made underboss to DeFede and Lastorino acted as *consigliere*. Amuso had been worried that, due to the weakened state of the Lucchese crime family, factions from within were eyeing his leadership, specifically the Bronx faction of the Lucchese organization. Feeling that he needed to showcase his power, Amuso ordered yet another attack. Powerful Bronx faction *capo* Aniello "Neil" Migliore was attending a party in a restaurant in Westbury, New York in 1992. Standing next to the front window of the building, Migliore was suddenly struck by bullets, which hit him in the head and chest. A gunman had driven past the restaurant and fired through the window at Migliore. He survived the attempt on his life, however, and, to the ire of Amuso, the attack did nothing to stop him from continuing operating in the Bronx crew. This tension with the Bronx faction of the organization was a key reason why Amuso made Crea underboss, as he had strong ties to the rising faction and Amuso hoped that this would keep them in line.

DeFede had been supervising the Lucchese crime family's garment district rackets since before his promotion to acting Boss, reportedly earning the organization "$40,000 per month" ("Joseph DeFede: American mobster," 2023). DeFede also placed his new underboss Crea in charge of the organization's construction and labor racketeering operations. DeFede could not have known the effect that this decision would have on him, but suffice to say that putting Crea in charge of these operations was the beginning of the end of DeFede's time as acting Boss. Crea expanded the rackets he was put in charge of, increasing the Lucchese crime family's profits to around $500,000 annually.

For a time, the organization operated with little trouble, with Amuso firmly in power whilst DeFede and Crea ran his rackets for him. Then, two events occurred almost simultaneously. First, after continued pressure from law enforcement throughout the mid-to-late 1990s, DeFede was arrested on nine counts of racketeering stemming from his overseeing of the organization's operations in the garment district. He pled guilty and was sentenced to nine years in prison. Second, Crea's success in running the construction and labor rackets convinced Amuso that DeFede had been skimming profits off the top for himself. Further to this, Amuso was furious with DeFede's guilty plea and, by the late 1990s, "Amuso's relationship with DeFede began to sour" ("Joseph DeFede: American mobster," 2023). When Amuso then replaced DeFede with Crea as acting Boss, profits continued to rise, cementing Amuso's belief that DeFede had been cheating him. Amuso decided that DeFede would pay with his life.

In February of 2002, DeFede was released from prison. Learning that Amuso had marked him for death, DeFede almost instantly switched alliances and became a government informant. Providing details to authorities regarding the numerous criminal rackets run by the Lucchese crime family, DeFede assisted in the eventual convictions of a plethora of Lucchese crime family members, including *capos*, soldiers, associates, and even some of his fellow leaders. When testifying, DeFede claimed that "he only earned $1,014,000, or approximately £250,000 per year, during his tenure as acting Boss." He put this amount in perspective when he stated, "a low-ranking family soldier would make an average $50,000 per year" ("Joseph DeFede: American mobster," 2023). After his work with law enforcement was over, DeFede and his wife entered the Witness Protection Program, taking on new identities and moving to Florida. In 2012, DeFede died from a heart attack.

Steven Crea

Steven "Stevie" Crea (his later nickname would be "Wonderboy") was born in 1947, growing up on Arthur Avenue in the Bronx. Like many mobsters before him, Crea's formative years were surrounded by the presence of organized crime. In his 20's, Crea worked closely with Genovese crime family member Vincent DiNapoli, who mentored him. The two were in the construction industry, and they "began working with the South East Bronx Community Organization (SEBCO)," which was created and run by the Catholic priest and brother to the Genovese crime family Boss Vincent Gigante, Louis (Bastone, 2020). SEBCO ran and maintained low-income housing and received funding from the federal government.

As Crea and DiNapoli operated in construction and shared an organized crime link to the Genovese family, they were awarded millions of dollars of contracts from SEBCO, which proved very profitable for the pair. At some point during the early 1980s, Crea was inducted into the Lucchese crime family under Anthony Corallo, where he would soon impress his superiors with his knack for making profit. In 1983, Crea's mentor DiNapoli was sent to prison. Crea, clearly having formed a strong bond with DiNapoli, visited him numerous times during his incarceration. Crea, who was godfather to DiNapoli's daughter, helped her to plan her wedding in her father's absence. Crea also took full control over their shared construction business with SEBCO. In 1985, Crea was convicted on a murder conspiracy charge. Authorities believed that Crea plotted to kill a man from the Bronx who Crea suspected had assaulted his wife. Two years later, however, the conviction was overturned.

In 1990, Crea was promoted to *capo* of the Bronx crew by Lucchese crime family Boss Amuso. Crea heavily invested himself in labor racketeering, with these operations quickly becoming a specialty of his. As *capo*, he and his crew took control of local branches of workers' unions such as the United Brotherhood of Carpenters and the Cement and Concrete Workers Union. He used his influence here to extort contractors all over New York City, with lucrative results for both himself and the Lucchese crime family. Crea also held a no-show job at one of the largest drywall contractors in the area. Crea's star was rising and in 1993, he was promoted by Amuso (who was by this point in prison) as underboss to DeFede. Before Crea could put his talents into action, however, he first had to dodge a conspiracy from within the organization to murder him. Amuso had been struggling with the Bronx faction of the Lucchese crime family, who he felt were maneuvering to take control, considering that he was imprisoned.

Crea, Bronx-born and formerly respected *capo* of the crew, was promoted to underboss in an attempt to quell the troublesome faction. However, Crea's ascension proved to cause more harm than good, as it almost sparked a civil war within the Lucchese crime family. Crea, along with acting Boss DeFede, decided to move the power center of the organization from Brooklyn to the Bronx, which had been the seat of the Lucchese family for years prior. Anthony Casso, who was still in hiding and had yet to be apprehended at this time, was outraged at this move. George Zappola and Frank Gioia Jr., who were Brooklyn loyalists, plotted to murder Crea and take control of the family for themselves. They had planned to lure Crea to a sit-down before murdering him, but this plot never materialized as, in 1993, Casso and his conspirators were caught by law enforcement and imprisoned on multiple charges.

From 1997 to 1999, Crea led the Lucchese crime family's "Construction Group." This entity was tasked with overseeing the payments received from contractors and settling disputes around the control of specific construction sites. The entity also organized a tax fraud scheme where they would put mobsters on company payrolls in order for them to declare legitimate taxable income to the IRS. Whilst in operation, the "Construction Group" controlled $40 million in construction contracts. 1998 saw Crea's ultimate promotion as, when DeFede was indicted on racketeering charges, Amuso made him acting Boss. During his time at the top of the Lucchese crime family, Crea began really showing off his talent for making profit, and the organization saw an extensive increase in its annual turnover. In fact, it was Crea's talent for money that convinced Amuso that previous acting Boss DeFede was skimming money off the top of the organization's racket profits, leading to a hit being placed on DeFede. As acting Boss, Crea also formed an alliance with the Gambino crime family, doing what he did best, extorting the officials of various labor unions. In 1999, Crea and an associate discussed their extortion activities with Sean Richard, son-in-law to Boss of the DeCavalcante crime family and John Riggi. It transpired that, throughout the conversation, Richard had been wearing a wire. In 2000, Crea (along with the other members of the "Construction Group") was indicted on extortion and racketeering charges related to his role in overseeing the Lucchese crime family's construction rackets. During the trial, it was revealed that those involved in the rackets had siphoned millions of dollars from both public and private projects within the construction industry. Crea would use his mobster muscle to extort contractors in order to create favorable contracts for the organization's sites. In 2001, he was convicted and sentenced to five years, eventually being released in 2006.

Louis "Louie Bagels" Daidone

With another acting Boss imprisoned, Amuso again had to fill the gap. He chose Louis "Louie Bagels" Daidone to replace Crea. Born in Bensonhurst, Brooklyn, in 1946, Daidone was a keen American football player. He played as a quarter-back for the team at New Utrecht High School and was offered a football scholarship with Indiana State University in 1963. It makes one wonder what could have been had Daidone accepted this opportunity.

However, as one may have deduced, he did not take the scholarship, choosing to stay in Bensonhurst. Daidone went on to operate multiple illegal rackets out of a bagel shop he owned called "Bagels by the Bay," hence his nickname "Louie Bagels." Daidone also owned a car servicing business, was involved in the highjacking of cigarettes, and worked as an associate of Paul Vario's crew.

In 1982, Daidone was inducted into the Lucchese crime family, alongside Alphonse D'Arco, in a ceremony presided over by then-Boss Anthony Corallo. Daidone was key in acting upon Amuso's near-constant assassination orders. In 1988, Daidone was ordered to kill Lucchese crime family associate Thomas "Red" Gilmore as Amuso suspected that he was an informant, a suspicion that Amuso would continue to make a habit out of. Gilmore was a small-time car thief and ran a chopshop. Daidone and two associates "tailed… Gilmore to his home in Queens, then ran up behind him and shot him in the head and neck" (Federal Bureau of Investigation, 2023). Daidone was also involved in the murder of Bruno Facciola, along with Frank Lastorino and Richard Pagliarulo (Mafia Cops Stephen Caracappa and Louis Eppolito gave over information that Facciola was an informant). Whilst Daidone did not stab or shoot Facciola, he was the one to stuff a dead canary in the corpse's mouth (an Amuso staple warning of the consequences of informing), and Facciola's body "was found, days later, stuffed into the trunk of his own car" (Federal Bureau of Investigation, 2023). In early 1991, Daidone's quick ascension through the ranks of the Lucchese crime family began, as he was promoted to acting *capo* to replace D'Arco when he himself was promoted to acting Boss.

In May of 1992, Daidone, along with fellow Lucchese mobsters, were convicted of conspiring to rob an armored truck back in 1988, a crime in which they stole $1.2 million. For this conviction, Daidone was sentenced to five years in prison. He was paroled in 1996 under the condition that he did not speak to known criminals for a further three years. Daidone almost violated this parole term when he made contact with fellow Lucchese mobster Raymond Argentina. It was around this time that Daidone saw his second promotion in so many years to *consigliere*. In 2000, acting Boss Steven Crea was sentenced to prison on racketeering charges, prompting Amuso to yet again promote Daidone to acting Boss.

As the turn of the century saw the Lucchese crime family in a state of chaos as many of its members were either being indicted for crimes or imprisoned, Amuso appointed Daidone to keep at least a semblance of stability in the organization. Unfortunately for Amuso, Daidone's reign as acting Boss would be extremely short-lived. Almost instantly after his promotion, Daidone was charged along with 13 other organized crime members on racketeering and extortion charges linked to numerous New York City businesses, including a Long Island strip club called Sinderella. Daidone took on further charges in 2003 relating to the murders of Gilmore in

1989 and Facciolo in 1990. The prosecution called upon acting Boss-turned-informant Alphonse D'Arco to testify at Daidone's trial, which incriminated him greatly. A final round of charges in 2004 was the final nail in the coffin for Daidone, who was subsequently sentenced to life in prison. As of today, this is where he stays, locked up at the United States Penitentiary in Allenwood, Pennsylvania.

A Change in Tactic

After three separate acting Bosses in 12 years, two of which turned to law enforcement, Amuso assumedly felt that a change in tactic was needed. With this in mind, Amuso did not simply promote a new acting Boss to the top of the Lucchese crime family, instead favoring the assembling of a ruling panel of members to oversee the organization's operations. This idea was not necessarily a new one, as Amuso had installed a similar panel back when Alphonse D'Arco was serving as acting Boss. Whilst Amuso did this mainly to stifle D'Arco's power as he no longer trusted that D'Arco was loyal to him, the panel consisted of multiple high-ranking Lucchese crime family members who would discuss and agree on the best decisions for the organization. As if following a pattern, this panel would last around six years before dissipating, being replaced by more acting Bosses under Amuso. This would yet again throw the Lucchese crime family hierarchy into flux.

CHAPTER 9

TAKING BACK POWER: THE RULING PANEL AND MATTHEW MADONNA

After a disastrous period of two decades, littered with imprisoned leaders, cracking foundations, and the corpses of their own members, the Lucchese crime family was barely holding itself together. Its official Boss, Vittorio Amuso, had been imprisoned since the early 1990s and ruled awkwardly from his jail cell. His attempts to stabilize the organization through acting Bosses had failed miserably. Desperate to save the Lucchese crime family from falling apart completely, Amuso decided that a complete flip of the hierarchical structure was necessary if the organization was to survive. Besides, what was better than one leader, if not three? In this penultimate chapter, we will explore the members of the ruling panel that took over the Lucchese crime family operation, the history of Matthew Madonna as well as his rule over the organization, the return of Steven Crea to the playing field, and law enforcement's attempt to end the Lucchese crime family once and for all.

A Panel of Three

After the arrest and sentencing of acting Boss Louis Daidone, a ruling panel was set up by Amuso as an alternate way to run the Lucchese crime family. The panel consisted of three members who would oversee the activities and operations of the Lucchese crime family under orders from Amuso. Three *capos* were promoted to the panel: Aniello Migliore, Joseph DiNapoli, and Matthew Madonna. All three men had decorated careers within the Lucchese crime family, serving in leadership positions. Interestingly, Amuso appointed Migliore even after attempting to have him murdered 11 years previously when Migliore served as a powerful *capo* for the Bronx faction of the organization. After his "brush with death" at the hands of Amuso, Migliore "kept a much lower profile" but still sat on the panel despite both his tense history with Amuso and his advanced age (Dickson, 2019). DiNapoli had been a member of the Genovese crime family along with his brother Vincent (Vincent had been the mobster who mentored Steven Crea) but had become a *capo* in the Lucchese crime family by the late 1990s. Madonna had an extensive history with the organization, which will be delved into shortly. The ruling panel got started on pulling the Lucchese crime family back from the brink and consolidating its power in the Bronx. The panel also looked at replenishing its ranks after many years of heavy law enforcement scrutiny had left many Lucchese crime family members behind bars. It was reported that when the panel was first installed in 2003, the organization consisted of approximately 9 *capos* and 82 soldiers. At the time of the panel's dissolution, the organization had grown to around 100 members in total.

This period of growth, or better yet, regrowth, was a relatively stable one. The ruling panel managed to keep it this way for four years until the Lucchese hierarchy was again assaulted by the strong arm of law enforcement. In 2007, two of the three panel members, DiNapoli and Madonna, were arrested along with *capo* Ralph Perna and soldier Nicodemo Scarfo Jr. through a law enforcement investigation dubbed "Operation Heat." Through this investigation, it was discovered that the New Jersey strand of the Lucchese crime family controlled and operated an extensive illegal gambling, money laundering, and racketeering ring that stretched from New Jersey all the way to Costa Rica. The organization was pulling in $2.2 billion from the operation and was both an enormous victory for law enforcement and a devastating blow to the recovering Lucchese crime family.

The charges did not stop there, however, and authorities did not pull their punches. In 2009, three separate indictments were dropped at the Lucchese crime family's feet. The first and second indictments charged DiNapoli, Madonna, *capos* Anthony Croce and Andrew Disimone, along with around 45 other family members, with operating rackets that grossed almost $400 million and attempting to bribe undercover police officers to look past illegal poker parlors. The third indictment was smaller in scale, charting Croce along with soldiers Joseph Datello and Frank Datello for running loan sharking and bookmaking operations out of a bar on Staten Island. Due to two of its three members facing hefty criminal charges, the ruling panel was disbanded after just six years in existence, never managing to achieve its goal of reinvigorating the Lucchese crime family.

Madonna Takes Over

The first known fact about Matthew Madonna involves him serving prison time, which astute readers will recognize as something that will become a pattern. During the late 1950s, whilst imprisoned at Green Haven Correctional Facility in New York State, Madonna met a drug dealer from Harlem named Nicky Barnes. The two assumedly got along as, when they were both released back into the world, Madonna began supplying Barnes with heroin, using his car to deliver the narcotics, which were filling the car's trunk to the brim. Barnes would visit the car after a time and replace the narcotics with cash. Then, Madonna would return and drive away, a substantial amount of money filling the trunk. Madonna's arrangement with Barnes of "driving a car loaded with heroin meant for a drug kingpin" for Barnes to then sell worked well for both men (Scarpo, 2015).

That is, until 1975, when Madonna was caught and arrested. Barnes, on the other hand, went on to "find another supplier and kept going for another two years" (Scarpo, 2015). In 1976, Madonna was finally sentenced, receiving 30 years in federal prison. Not long after the start of his sentence, his prison term was extended by just over a year. In 1981, Madonna was pulled from his cell to testify in front of a grand jury regarding the drug trade in New York City. Madonna, seemingly taking the teachings of "honor among thieves" seriously, refused to say a word, even after being given immunity from self-incrimination. Due to his refusal to testify, "the judge held Madonna in contempt of court," thus his sentence was extended (Scarpo, 2015).

Released after serving 20 years, Madonna found himself back on the streets of New York City in 1995 and was now 60 years of age. It is clear that Madonna had no intention of leaving his criminal past behind him after his "heavy time" in prison as, in 1998, he was inducted into the Lucchese crime family, reported as a reward for his silence during his incarceration and to assist in refilling the organization's coffers (Scarpo, 2015).

It was not long before Madonna was promoted to the rank of *capo* and, after another stint in prison, was back acting as a *capo* for the Lucchese crime family in 2003. After acting Boss Louis Daidone was incarcerated, Madonna was appointed as one of three organization members to sit on the ruling panel tasked with overseeing the Lucchese crime family for Vittorio Amuso. Some reports "name Madonna as head of the panel," but this is disputed, as fellow panel member Migliore has been described as "more equal than the others" (Scarpo, 2015). After his arrest and numerous charges placed against him in 2009, the ruling panel was disbanded. However, Madonna was released on bail pending trial and was, therefore, free to take over as acting Boss of the Lucchese crime family. Since 2006, former underboss and acting Boss Steven Crea had been out on parole, with the condition that he was not to have contact with any known mobsters or union officials. These conditions expired in 2009, and, along with Madonna, Crea rejoined the leadership of the Lucchese crime family.

Bombarded With Charges

With Crea back with the organization and former panel member DiNapoli as his *consigliere*, Madonna was poised to bring the Lucchese crime family back to as it was in the glory days. However, instead of wealth, power, and respect, all that came to Madonna and his leadership were charges and indictments. In 2013, the FBI arrested individuals from various criminal organizations on racketeering charges relating to involvement in carting companies in three counties of New York and two counties of New Jersey.

The Lucchese, Gambino, and Genovese had formed somewhat of an alliance in this venture, maintaining control over waste disposal businesses and controlling who could pick up the waste and in what location. The alliance also muscled protection money out of the businesses to ensure no other extortion from other organized crime entities. It is interesting to note here that the last time the Lucchese, Gambino, and Genovese crime families formed an alliance was during a plot to take control of the Mafia Commission back in the 1950s. Although admittedly, this alliance did end in betrayal, so one can take this observation as one will.

In 2012, Crea ordered Lucchese soldiers Vincent Bruno and Paul Cassano to whack an associate of the Bonanno crime family who Crea believed had disrespected him. The two hitmen went to the Bonanno associate's home but, for reasons unknown at this point in time, the assassination was not completed. Another botched assassination order from Crea occurred in 2016 when he told soldier Joseph Detello to kill an informant over in New Hampshire, but Detello was unsuccessful as he was unable to find the target. The Lucchese crime family rank-and-file was not faring any better in regard to law enforcement scrutiny. Detello and fellow Lucchese crime family members were accused of operating a narcotics trafficking ring that moved products from South America over the border into the United States. The smuggling scheme reportedly brought five kilograms of cocaine, around one kilogram of heroin, and an extensive 1,000 kilograms of marijuana into the country.

A larger case that implemented both leadership and rank-and-file members came in regard to the 2013 shooting of Lucchese crime family associate Michael Meldish. Meldish was the leader of the "notorious Purple Gang, which back, in the 1970s and 1980s, dealt heroin in the Bronx and Harlem and whacked people for the Bonanno, Lucchese, and Genovese crime families" (Scarpo, 2015). The gang was brutal, with their calling card being "dismembering victims' bodies" (Scarpo, 2015). Associate Terrence Caldwell and soldier Christopher Londonio were the ones accused of actually carrying out the assassination, with Caldwell already being in custody for attempted murder (in 2013, he was accused of shooting Bonanno crime family soldier Enzo Stagno in the chest) when he was indicted in the Meldish killing. Allegedly, in November of 2013, "pulled to a stop at a crosswalk and was exiting his vehicle when he was fired on" (Scarpo, 2015). He was shot once in the head and died of his injuries. Acting Boss Madonna was also accused of involvement in the ordering of the murder, having been reported to be "angry at Meldish and his ways" (Scarpo, 2015). It is also entirely likely that Madonna and Meldish had some kind of long-standing relationship, seeing as though "when the Purple Gang was murdering and dismembering" during the 1970s, Madonna was running his heroin-supplying scheme (Scarpo, 2015).

In 2013, the FBI actually minimized the number of agents they had investigating the Five Families of New York. It is an arguable opinion that, by this time, the Five Families of New York were merely a shadow of their former selves during the mid-20th century and, considering the amount of convictions law enforcement had managed to make stick on family members since the 1990s, it is perhaps reasonable to suggest that this sparked the decision to pool resources elsewhere. Despite the minimization, the FBI still kept two teams (Squad C5 and Squad C16) to watch the Five Families of New York carefully. These two teams were 18-strong each, the former focusing on the Genovese, Bonanno, and Colombo crime families and the latter focusing on the Gambino and Lucchese crime families. The manpower of these teams was diminished, however, as, before the cutback, the FBI had teams of 10 to 20 agents investigating each of the Five Families. Cutting back on surveillance of the Five Families of New York did not seem to have an adverse effect on the rate of indictments, however. In May of 2017, the Lucchese crime family leadership, along with 16 other members and associates, were indicted and charged with a laundry list of crimes. The list of charges is as follows: racketeering, assault, attempted murder, illegal gambling, narcotics, firearms, armed robbery, fraud, murder, witness tampering, and the trafficking of contraband cigarettes. It is also potent to note that these charges were backdated to as early as 2000. In 2019, Joseph Datello pled guilty to all charges brought against him, receiving 14 years in prison. In the same year, Lucchese crime family *capo* and son of Crea Steven D. "Stevie Junior" Crea also pled guilty to charges including racketeering and murder conspiracy, for which he was sentenced to 13 years.

The Leadership Topples

With all this heat from law enforcement, the Lucchese crime family began to buckle under the pressure. The blow that cemented the organization's complete downfall came when its leadership, that being Madonna, Crea, and DiNapoli, were convicted. After his involvement in the murder of Michael Meldish came to light, Madonna was slapped with a life sentence in July 2020. In the face of all manner of convictions, Crea was also sentenced to life in the same year, as well as a fine of $400,000 and the forfeit of $1 million. DiNapoli, considering the sentences handed to his contemporaries, got off lightly. He received a sentence of 52 months in prison along with a fine of $250,000. DiNapoli was released from prison in January of 2023. With this, the leadership of the Lucchese crime family, as well as a good majority of its rank-and-file members, was well and truly extinguished. However, Vittorio Amuso was still stirring in his cell and, as long as he drew breath, he would not allow his organization to die. There is one final chapter to the history of the Lucchese crime family that brings the organization right into the world we live in today.

CHAPTER 10

RAN FROM BEHIND BARS: THE "MODERN" LUCCHESE CRIME FAMILY

Throughout this exploration, we have seen the Lucchese crime family shift between prosperity and ruin on numerous occasions. In the present, the organization has skulked back into the shadows and, in a sense, reverted back to the ways that the old Cosa Nostra mob bosses would be proud of, although under very different circumstances. However, Vittorio Amuso, "The Deadly Don" himself, is still sitting in his prison cell at the Federal Correctional Complex, Butner in North Carolina, and is running the Lucchese crime family with the same absolute power that he did when he was a free man. Whilst the tone of this section so far perhaps indicates that the Lucchese crime family is no more, it must be stated clearly that this is not the case. Indeed, Amuso has made sure that the organization has leadership and, consequently, is still a very real threat that has its influences permeating throughout modern society. In fact, it may well be a positive for the Lucchese crime family that its Boss is locked up states away from where it runs its operations, as this creates a false sense of security in both law enforcement and public discourse. This imagined safety is what the organization needs to lick its wounds and recuperate whilst eyes look to other things. When and if the Lucchese crime family regains its power, it will be back to its old ways before anyone gets a chance to react. In this final chapter, we will explore the newest iteration of the Lucchese crime family's leadership, the current criminal investigations involving the organization, and the continued effect of the criminal family on our society today.

The New Hierarchy

In May of 2019, the trial of former Lucchese crime family soldier Eugene "Boobsie" Castelle was ongoing. Castelle was being charged with racketeering and running an illegal gambling business. As a witness, the prosecution called John Pennisi to the stand, also a former Lucchese crime family soldier, but now turned government witness. Throughout his testimony, Pennisi revealed extensive details regarding the current state of his former organization, giving those present a clear picture of the state of the Lucchese crime family.

Inducted into the Lucchese crime family in 2013, Pennisi's ceremony was not particularly grand, occurring in the basement of a house in Staten Island. He was sworn into the organization by acting Boss Matthew Madonna and *capo* John Castellucci. Pennisi never rose up the ranks of the family, working as a soldier with the Brooklyn faction of the organization, who had their base in Tottenville, Staten Island. After a few years, Pennisi "flipped" and began working with the FBI. One can assume that this was either because of the immense pressure from law enforcement that the organization was under at the time or perhaps Pennisi wanted out due to the unstable Amuso, who insisted on accusing individuals of being informants.

Regardless of his reasons, Pennisi began cooperating with law enforcement, going on to testify in the trials of many of his former allies. What was learned from Pennisi at the trial is as follows. Back in 2017, the Brooklyn faction of the Lucchese crime family wrote a letter to imprisoned Boss Vittorio Amuso. The letter seeped frustration, as the faction was outraged that the seat of power for the Lucchese crime family had slowly been moving from Brooklyn over to the Bronx. As an aside, the Bronx had been the historical seat of power for the organization before shifting over to Brooklyn. When Steven Crea was made the underboss of Joseph DeFede, the two planned to make the Bronx the central seat of power once again. Although tensions arose from this, which almost ended in a civil war within the Lucchese crime family, the tension died down over time, and the movement of power to the Bronx had been slowly transpiring since.

Being resistant to the movement of power over to the Bronx originally, Amuso wrote a letter to then-underboss Crea, which ordered that Brooklyn-based mobster Michael "Big Mike" DeSantis would replace Matthew Madonna as acting Boss of the organization. The letter also mentioned that if the Bronx faction resisted the change, then Amuso would order the assassinations of multiple *capos* and soldiers within the faction. With the letter, Amuso had sent a hitlist with the names of those who would be targeted written on it. Additionally, those present at the trial learned that the modern Lucchese crime family operates with seven crews: two on Long Island, two in the Bronx, one in Manhattan, one in New Jersey, and one that moves between Brooklyn and Staten Island.

As stated, Pennisi has drawn back the curtain on the Lucchese crime family, as well as its continued politics and friction. However, there is one element to Pennisi that is interesting to note. Earlier in this section, we mused over Pennisi's reasoning as to why he turned informant. Well, Pennisi had publicly stated what made him turn to law enforcement, and the reason is unique, to say the least. Pennisi claims to have got an "earth-shaking message from the great beyond via his deceased grandparents that convinced him to become a government turncoat" (Capeci, 2021). Pennisi went on to state that he received this paranormal message "just as he was praying to a photo of his late grandparents and seeking their advice about whether he should turn informant" (Capeci, 2021). The problem that comes with Pennisi's supernatural revelation is that, during his testimonies against Castelle and two other Lucchese crime family members, he failed to mention this, always maintaining that "he flipped after Lucchese family leaders wrongly tagged him as a rat" (Capeci, 2021). Two attorneys who represented defendants that Pennili testified against are furious that they were not able to ask him about these paranormal encounters in front of a jury, stating, "It is simply inexcusable that the defense were never told about… the paranormal events that he claims triggered his cooperation. Had these materials, and the many other things now revealed by Pennisi, been properly disclosed by the government, no grand jury or trial jury would ever credit his tales" (Capeci, 2021). The attorneys ended their attack on Pennisi's character by stating, "His capitalizing on his cooperation calls into question his prior testimony and his motives to fabricate now" (Capeci, 2021).

Previously, Pennisi had specified that he went informant as he feared for his life, explaining in detail what he experienced prior to joining witness protection. Pennisi describes being "chased by five or six Bloods at a Manhattan job site" (Capeci, 2021), going on to state that the Lucchese clan "had started using other ethnic groups. They began using the Bloods" (Capeci, 2021). These encounters served to "underscore his [Pennisi's] uneasiness due to mixed messages he was getting from the family's acting boss Michael 'Big Mike' DeSantis" (Capeci, 2021). Pennisi also credited his son for his decision to flip, describing his son, "who lost 17 years without his father during the years Pennisi was in prison for killing a neighborhood rival", as "a nervous wreck" (Capeci, 2021). After mulling the decision to contact the FBI over, Pennisi claims that his son told him that he "thought he should go tomorrow," to which Pennisi agreed to do. It seems that, with his talk of the supernatural, Pennisi has put doubt in minds about what he has testified regarding the Lucchese crime family. Of course, one can make their own decision about whether they believe Pennisi or not, but what is clear is that there is a debate to be had regarding the validity of his claims.

Continuing Criminal Investigations

Despite the battering that the Lucchese crime family received from law enforcement from the 1990s onward, there are still various criminal investigations into the organization happening in the modern day. In March of 2018, a family soldier named Dominick Capelli, along with nine associates, were arrested.

The law enforcement operation (named Operation "The Vig Is Up") uncovered one of the largest loan sharking operations ever investigated by the United States Attorney General's Office. Capelli's scheme involved making individuals (over 47 people in this case) who took out loans pay a highly inflated interest percentage, averaging over 200% annually, which created a debt trap that loanees were unable to escape. The operation was alleged to be run out of New Rochelle in New York and in the Bronx, with the defendants also accused of running an extremely lucrative bookmaking operation in parallel with the loan sharking.

In 2018, another Lucchese crime family soldier, one Anthony Grado, was arrested for forcing a doctor to prescribe them a large amount of Oxycodone pills, presumably to sell at street level. Grado had assistance in this from associate Lawrence "Fat Larry" Tranese, and the pair harassed and assaulted the doctor from 2011 to 2013. In one instance, the doctor "was stabbed by a Lucchese associate on Grado's orders" (Bain, 2018). Using wiretaps and hidden cameras, authorities were able to catch Grado and Tranese in the act, with Grado recorded threatening, "If the prescriptions go in anybody's hands besides mine, I'll put a bullet right in your head" (Bain, 2018). Grado was also recorded "telling the hapless doctor that he would feed him 'to the [expletive] lions' if he wrote prescriptions without the mob's permission" (Bain, 2018). Both men pled guilty and were sentenced to prison, 12 years for Grado and 3 years for Tranese, and fined "up to $1 million" (Bain, 2018).

Of the crime, a high-ranking FBI agent stated, "Organized crime groups and other criminal entities are seizing on the outbreak of addiction plaguing our country to make money. It shouldn't be a shock that members of the Lucchese crime family used violence to force a member of the medical community to further their criminal enterprise" (Bain, 2018). A more mysterious investigation began in October of 2018 when an associate of the Lucchese crime family

Vincent Zito was found dead in his home in Brooklyn. Zito had suffered two bullet wounds to the back of the head and a handgun was resting next to his body. Zito has been alleged to have been a loan shark, and his brother Anthony (imprisoned for extortion in 1971) was a known associate of Boss Vittorio Amuso. This investigation is still ongoing as of now.

In December of 2020, organized crime and reality television collided spectacularly when Lucchese crime family soldier John Perna was charged with the aggravated assault of the husband of reality television star Dina Cantin. Cantin had been a cast member of the show *The Real Housewives of New Jersey*. It was uncovered that Perna had been hired to carry out the attack by Cantin's ex-husband Thomas Manzo. Manzo and his family had been facing accusations of having mob ties since 1983 when "Albert 'Tiny' Manzo Sr. was executed gangland-style in August" of that year (Kennedy, 2020). Albert, who was Manzo's father, was "found in the trunk of his Lincoln Continental outside a supermarket in Hillside, New Jersey: naked, his arms and legs tied with plastic, with four bullet holes in his torso" (Kennedy, 2020). Perna had accepted in return for a discount price for his own wedding reception. This wedding reception went ahead "about a month later and was attended by about 330 people, including members of the Lucchese family" (Kennedy, 2020). In September of 2022, five Lucchese crime family members and associates were accused of running an extensive illegal gambling operation. The accused (soldier Anthony Villani and associates James Coumoutsos, Dennis Filizzola, Michael Praino, and Louis Tucci Jr.) all faced charges, including racketeering and attempted extortion, among others.

The Lucchese Crime Family Today

As learned in Pennisi's testimony during Castelle's trial, the current acting Boss of the Lucchese crime family is Michael "Big Mike" DeSantis. DeSantis "got to the top of the hill in an unusual way: a letter from his imprisoned-for-life predecessor Vic Amuso" telling him that he was now in charge of the Lucchese crime family (Amoruso, 2019). However, now that he is on the radar of law enforcement, they are "watching him closely to see what he does with it" (Amoruso, 2019). DeSantis had a journey into the Lucchese crime family, not unlike many others, being inducted into the organization in the late 1980s. The ceremony was presided over by a cavalcade of recognizable names such as Anthony Casso, Alphonse D'Arco, and Amuso himself. He "came up in a crew run by 'Fat Pete' Chiodo" and set about proving himself. (Amoruso, 2019). Not long after DeSantis' induction, "Chiodo received a contract to murder John Morrissey, a business agent for Local 580 of the Ornamental Ironworkers Union" (Amoruso, 2019). It transpired that Morrissey had assisted in a large racketeering scheme run in conjunction between all of the Five Families of New York involving the fitting of windows at inflated prices. Amuso and his underboss Casso were "afraid that Morrissey would cooperate with authorities," so they marked him for death" (Amoruso, 2019).

Completing the hit, Chiodo dragged the body of the union leader outside to find DeSantis "digging a hole with a backhoe. The men threw in the body and covered it up with dirt" (Amoruso, 2019). After this work impressed his superiors, DeSantis became "the favored hitman for Amuso and Casso," even tasking him with "the murder of acting boss Alphonse D'Arco, who they suspected would become an informant" (Amoruso, 2019). D'Arco was lured to a meeting at the Kimberley Hotel in Manhattan. It was actually DeSantis' presence at the meeting that put D'Arco onto the assassination attempt, as the meeting was for high-ranking Lucchese crime family members and, DeSantis was a soldier. Also, "the pistol bulging from DeSantis' back was a big tip-off" and D'Arco fled, avoiding his would-be assassins (Amoruso, 2019). DeSantis was put in prison due to D'Arco turning informant and, unlike D'Arco, "kept his mouth shut and did his time" (Amoruso, 2019).

In 2010, he was released from prison and returned to the streets as not only "a capable killer, but as a stand-up guy" (Amoruso, 2019). Not long after DeSantis' release came, the letter exclaiming him as the new acting Boss of the Lucchese crime family arrived, and since "despite being locked up for life, Amuso's word [is] still law on the streets of New York," Madonna and Crea stepped aside to make room for DeSantis (Amoruso, 2019). So, Michael "Big Mike" DeSantis is now the acting Boss of the Lucchese crime family, along with Patty "Red" Dellorusso as his underboss and Andrew DeSimone as his *consigliere*. It seems only time will tell if he can raise the organization back into a place of profit, respect, and power, or whether he will simply bide his time, waiting for the opportune moment when his organization is again ready to extend its influence throughout New York City and beyond.

CONCLUSION

Looking back at the journey through the history of the Lucchese crime family, as well as the history of the American Mafia as a whole, we have experienced a plethora of different elements in a wide berth of contexts. In the breeding grounds of late 19th and early 20th century New York City, we saw the beginnings of the American Mafia, tearing into existence as small and disorganized gangs before stitching together to form larger fabrics that would ultimately become the tapestry that is the American Mafia. In the prosperity of the mid-20th century, we saw the formation of the Five Families of New York, as well as the Mafia Commission, born from the decision that crime required self-governance if it were to not only survive, but prosper. Toward the end of the 20th century, we saw the brutality of organized crime as different groups clashed with threats from both the outside and inside, threatening to tear the institutions apart at the seams. At the turn of the century, we saw an old beast attempt to learn new tricks, adapting to its surroundings with varying levels of success. The history of organized crime is an intricate and complex one, full of shifting morality, brutal exchanges, and dire consequences. Through experiencing all of this, one hopes to have gained a foundational understanding of the complexities of organized crime in the United

States and, by doing so, is able to further explore using the knowledge learned here to stand on in order to reach new heights.

In regard to the Lucchese crime family, it seems clear from this exploration that the organization's success and effectiveness came in ebbs and flows. From the lucrative expansions of the two Tommies (Lucchese and Gagliano), the violent paranoia of the Amuso-Casso era, the change in the state of play from Alphonse D'Arco's switch of allegiance, and the enormous mistake of Anthony Corallo in his Jaguar, the Lucchese crime family is a dichotomy in of itself. It harbors one of the most stable and peaceful periods of any Five Family organization, yet also one of the most violent and brutal. Its namesake Tommy Lucchese can quite easily be considered one of the most important figures in American Mafia history, helping to pave the way for organized crime in the United States and creating codes and values that any self-respecting mob boss should follow to the letter. That being said, it also spawned the likes of Vittorio Amuso and Anthony Casso who, although fiercely intelligent, were blinded by both the acquisition of power and, indeed, the protection of it and, in doing so, allowed paranoia to fester to the point of causing them to commit a pseudo-genocide within their own ranks. When all is said and done, the Lucchese crime family is arguably one of the most intriguing Mafia organizations to ever exist, constantly shifting and growing in unexpected ways from its birth in the 1910s up until the modern day. The Lucchese crime family is a story that is still being told and, whatever it comes up with, we can be sure it will be gripping to experience.

With that, it feels correct to end on a quote from French economist and writer Frederic Bastiat, which truly invites one to ponder on the human condition, especially when one contextualizes it within the sphere of organized crime:

When plunder becomes a way of life for a group of men in a society, over the course of time they create for themselves a legal system that authorizes it and a moral code that glorifies it. –Frederic Bastiat

REFERENCES

Amoruso, D. (2019, June 17). Meet the new boss: Profile of Lucchese Mafia family leader Michael "Big Mike" DeSantis. *Gangsters Inc*. https://gangstersinc.org/profiles/blogs/profile-of-lucchese-mafia-family-boss-michael-big-mike-desantis

Bain, J. (2018, April 6). *Mob threatened doctor to write scripts for 230K Oxycodone pills: feds*. New York Post. https://nypost.com/2018/04/05/mob-threatened-doctor-to-write-scripts-for-230k-oxycodone-pills-feds/

Bastone, W. (2020, December 15). *The priest and the mob*. The Village Voice. https://www.villagevoice.com/2020/12/15/the-priest-and-the-mob/

Bruno, J. (2022, November). *Joe Morello and the Black Handers – Legends of America*. Www.legendsofamerica.com. https://www.legendsofamerica.com/20th-blackhand/

Bush, L. (2015, November 27). *November 27: Barnett Baff and the Poultry Racket*. Jewish Currents. https://jewishcurrents.org/november-27-barnett-baff-and-the-poultry-racket

Capeci, J. (2021, June 4). *Mobster John Pennisi said spirit of his grandparents told him to turn rat*. New York Post.

https://nypost.com/2021/06/04/mobster-john-pennisi-said-spirit-of-his-grandparents-told-him-to-turn-rat/

Chase, D. (1999, January 10). *The Sopranos* [TV]. HBO.

Celona, L. (2020, October 25). *NYPD's notorious "Mob Cops" saga becoming true-crime TV series.* The New York Post. https://nypost.com/2020/10/25/nypds-notorious-mob-cops-saga-becoming-true-crime-tv-series/

Cipollini, C. (2017, July 13). *Don't dare call him "Three Finger Brown."* The Mob Museum. https://themobmuseum.org/blog/lucchese-three-finger-brown-death-anniversary/

Dickson, M. (2013, July 8). *Tommy Gagliano - The Quiet Don.* American Mafia History. https://americanmafiahistory.com/tommy-gagliano/

Dickson, M. (2015, September 21). *Carmine Tramunti - Financier of The French Connection.* American Mafia History. https://americanmafiahistory.com/carime-tramunti/

Dickson, M. (2019, October 12). *Aniello Migliore - A respected and highly regarded member of the Lucchese family.* American Mafia History. https://americanmafiahistory.com/anielle-migliore-a-respected-and-highly-regarded-member-of-the-lucchese-family/

Dunn, M. (2021, August 18). *How one fateful meeting on a farm in Upstate New York caused the downfall of the Mafia* (A. Farley, Ed.). All That's Interesting. https://allthatsinteresting.com/apalachin-meeting

Faddah, A. (2020, February 21). *The former Five Points neighborhood where Luciano grew up after coming from Sicily, and met his lifelong friends and criminal associates.* Blogs.shu.edu. https://blogs.shu.edu/nyc-history/2020/02/21/castellammarese-war/

Federal Bureau of Investigation. (2023). *Acting Luchese Family Boss sentenced to life.* FBI. https://archives.fbi.gov/archives/news/stories/2004/july/canary_070604

Feuer, A. (2000, September 1). *Anthony Corallo, Mob Boss, dies in federal prison at 87.* The New York Times. https://www.nytimes.com/2000/09/01/nyregion/anthony-corallo-mob-boss-dies-in-federal-prison-at-87.html

Frankenheimer, J. (Director). (1975, May 21). *French Connection II* [Film]. 20th Century Fox.

Frédéric Bastiat. (n.d.). Www.goodreads.com. https://www.goodreads.com/quotes/6862167-when-plunder-becomes-a-way-of-life-for-a-group

Friedkin, W. (Director). (1971, October 7). *The French Connection* [Film]. 20th Century Fox.

Gaetano Reina. (2020). Timenote.info. https://timenote.info/en/Gaetano-Reina

Guide to Senate Records: Chapter 18 1946-1968. (2016, August 15). National Archives. https://www.archives.gov/legislative/guide/senate/chapter-18-1946-1968.html#18E-7

Harlem World Magazine. (2023). *East Harlem's Tommy Lucchese founding member of the Italian Mafia 1899 – 1967*. Harlem World Magazine. https://www.harlemworldmagazine.com/east-harlems-tommy-lucchese-founding-member-of-the-italian-mafia-1899-1967/

How did Salvatore Maranzano get killed? - Death Photos. (2023). National Crime Syndicate. https://www.nationalcrimesyndicate.com/salvatore-maranzano-death/

Joseph DeFede: American mobster (1934 - 2012); Mobster, Criminal, Gangster; from: United States of America | Biography, facts, information, career, wiki, life. (n.d.). Peoplepill.com. https://peoplepill.com/people/joseph-defede

Joseph Pinzolo. (2023). *Academic Dictionaries and Encyclopedias*. https://en-academic.com/dic.nsf/enwiki/1919672

Kennedy, D. (2020, July 4). *Inside the Mob ties that plague RHONJ star Dina Manzo's family*. New York Post. https://nypost.com/2020/07/04/inside-the-mob-ties-that-plague-rhonj-star-dina-manzos-family/

Knight, M. (2021, April 17). *The Commission trial lifted the lid on the New York Mafia*. The Mob Museum. https://themobmuseum.org/blog/the-commission-trial-lifted-the-lid-on-the-new-york-mafia/

Lucky Luciano (n.d.) National Crime Syndicate. https://www.nationalcrimesyndicate.com/famous-mobster-quotes/

Lubasch, A. H. (1985, February 27). *U.S. INDICTMENT SAYS 9 GOVERNED NEW YORK MAFIA*. The New York Times. https://www.nytimes.com/1985/02/27/nyregion/us-indictment-says-9-governed-new-york-mafia.html

Marchant, A. (2012). The French Connection: Between myth and reality. *Revue D'Histoire, 115*(3), 89–102. Cairn. https://www.cairn-int.info/article-E_VIN_115_0089--the-french-connection-between-myths.htm

Margaritoff, M. (2021, December 16). *"All he wanted to do is kill": The bloody story of Mafia hitman Anthony "Gaspipe" Casso (A. Farley, Ed.).* All That's Interesting. https://allthatsinteresting.com/anthony-casso

Oxford University Press. (1989). The Oxford English Dictionary (2nd ed.). Clarendon Press; Oxford.

Petepiece, A. (2018). *MAFIA COMMISSION : a history of the board of directors of la cosa nostra*. Tellwell Talent. https://www.amazon.co.uk/Mafia-Commission-History-Directors-Nostra/dp/0228806704?asin=0228806704&revisionId=&format=4&depth=1

Plain Sight Productions. (2020, December 30). *The French Connection*. Medium. https://plainsightprod.medium.com/the-french-connection-8044231bf0c3

Raab, S. (2006). *The rise, decline, and resurgence of America's most powerful Mafia empires*. Robson.

Reppetto, T. (2009). *American Mafia : a history of its rise to power*. Mjf Books.

Robbins, T., & Capeci, J. (2019, March 28). *Mob boss who inspired other infamous turncoats dies in witness protection.* The New York Post. https://nypost.com/2019/03/28/mob-boss-who-inspired-other-infamous-turncoats-dies-in-witness-protection/

Scarpo, E. (2015, December 13). *Lucchese Boss Matty Madonna's longtime criminal career.* Cosa Nostra News. https://www.cosanostranews.com/2015/12/lucheses-allied-with-bloods-affiliated.html

Scorsese, M. (Director). (1990, September 19). *Goodfellas* [Film]. Warner Bros. Pictures.

Scorsese, M. (Director). (2006, October 6). *The Departed* [Film]. Warner Bros. Pictures.

The New York Times. (1930, February 27). Wealthy Ice Dealer Shot in Doorway; Gaetano Reina Shot Down as He Left Apartment He Had in Addition to Bronx Home. *The New York Times.* https://www.nytimes.com/1930/02/27/archives/wealthy-ice-dealer-slain-in-doorway-gaetano-reina-shot-down-as-he.html

Tommy Lucchese. (2023). The Mob Museum. https://themobmuseum.org/notable_names/tommy-lucchese/

Tosches, N. (2013, November 7). *The American Mafia started in New Orleans.* Delancey Place. https://delanceyplace.com/view-archives.php?p=2290

www.ingramcontent.com/pod-product-compliance
Lightning Source LLC
Chambersburg PA
CBHW071352080526
44587CB00017B/3077